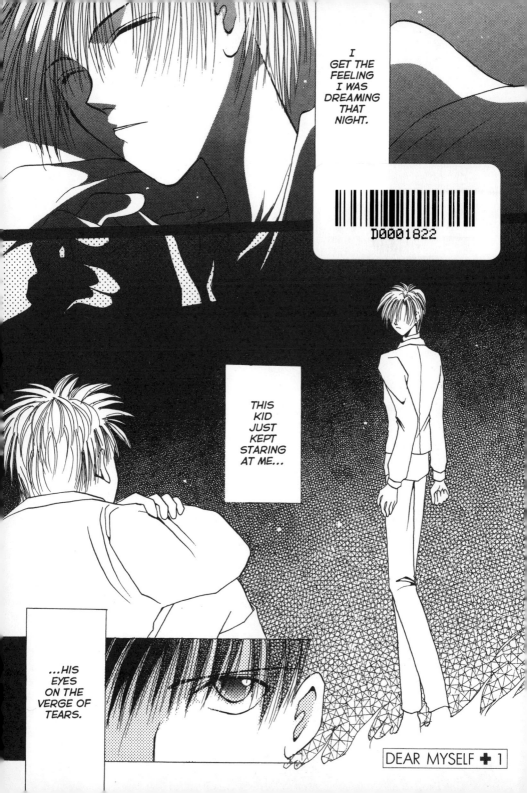

I GET THE FEELING I WAS DREAMING THAT NIGHT.

THIS KID JUST KEPT STARING AT ME...

...HIS EYES ON THE VERGE OF TEARS.

DEAR MYSELF ✚ 1

DON'T CRY...
...I'M RIGHT HERE...
DEAR MYSELF, 1
ディア・マイセルフ

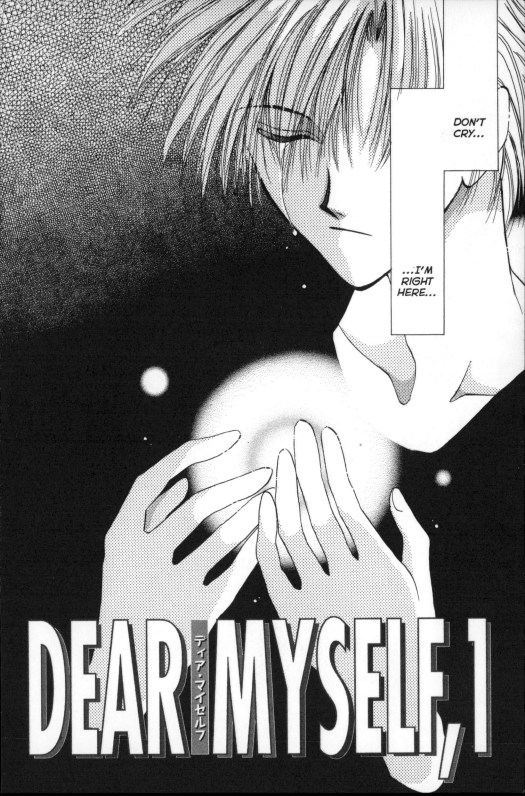

BRRINNG
BRRINNG
shff...
ごそ...
MMNF...
ぱしっ
THAP
...
MORNING...?

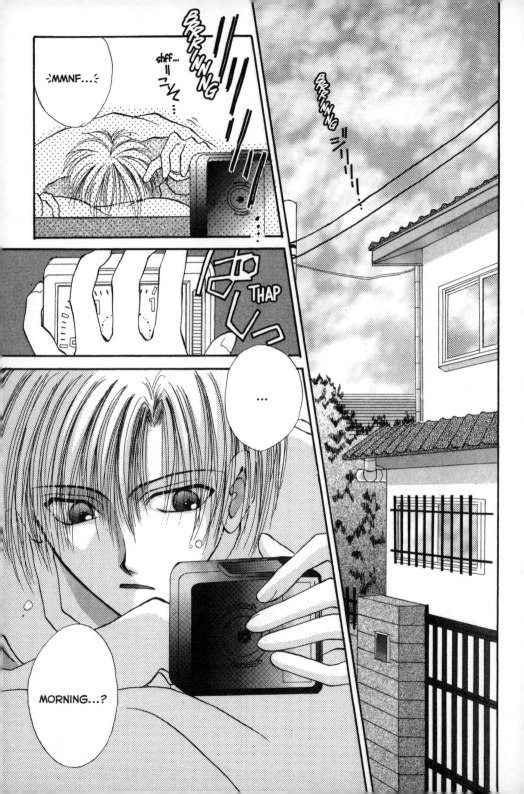

FEELS LIKE I SLEPT REALLY GREAT...
HUH?
NNNG--
IS IT JUST ME, OR IS MY ROOM ARRANGED KINDA WEIRD?
?
?
STUPID BANGS... WHAT'S UP WITH...
ばんっ
SLAM
HIROFUMI!
YOU ALL AWAKE? YOU'RE GONNA BE LATE!
DAMMIT, CHIKA!!
KNOCK BEFORE YOU BUST INTO SOMEONE'S...
...ROOM...?!

YOU... ARE CHIKA... RIGHT?
HUH?!
WELL, DUH! WHAT'S WRONG?
This some new way of being a pain in the butt?
NO, IT'S JUST...
...I THOUGHT YOU WERE MORE BOYISH...
What the?
....
KNOCK IT OFF.
NO FEVER...
MAYBE YOUR EYESIGHT JUST SUCKED UNTIL TODAY?
I've looked like this for a while now.
Hrm...
MM-... MAYBE?
OKAY, COME ON AND GET DRESSED.
?!
thff

WHAT'S THIS?
UH, YOUR UNI-FORM?
WHAT'RE YOU TALKIN' ABOUT?
WHERE'S MY HIGH-COLLAR JACKET?
MO-O-OM Hirofumi's gone crazy!
ZOOM
AAAH!
CHIKA?!
WHAT THE HELL ...?!
THIS SORTA THING HAPPEN A LOT...?
DID I FALL INTO SOME OTHER DIMENSION WHEN I WASN'T LOOKING...?
...OR HAS MY FAMILY BEEN TAKEN OVER BY ALIENS...?!!
BM-BMP
BM-BMP
BM-BMP

YEAH, RIGHT...
Sigh
ふっ...
ばんっ
BAM
どたどたどた
THMP THMP THMP
HIROFUMI?!
CAN IT BE YOU'VE...
OH.
MOM...
DANG, YOU'VE GOTTEN OLD.
Sshp
DOES MY DARLING SON HAVE A DEATH WISH?
Ho! Ho! Ho!
NO, IT... IT HAS TO BE!
ALL THOSE ODD STATEMENTS...
THAT RUDE SPEECH ...!!
Thmp Thmp
Y-YIKES...
I was just telling the truth...
HIROFUMI!
YOUR MEMORY'S COME BACK!
WHAT?

HUH?
WHA?
QUESTION FOR YOU, BIG BROTHER!!
WHAT'S TODAY'S DATE, YEAR AND ALL?
びっ POINT
I'm so happy, and yet... it's too bad...
Um...
MAY 13, 1995...
BZZZT! HERE, TAKE A LOOK AT THIS.
ばさ
FLAFF
1997年(平成9年)4月26日(土曜日)
プラス創刊
WHAT THE ...?!
どーん...
DUN-DUNN
HUH?
WHAT?
1997 ...?
OKAY, BIG BROTHER ...
...QUIT FREAKIN' AND JUST LISTEN UP.

UNTIL TODAY, HIROFUMI...
...FOR THE LAST TWO YEARS, YOU'VE HAD AMNESIA!
WHAT...?
HERE'S WHAT YOU LOOK LIKE NOW, BY THE WAY.
FWIP
GAAAH!
MY HEAD LOOKS LIKE A SUSHI MAT!
OKAY, WAIT A SEC...
...JUST WHAT THE HELL IS GOING ON?!
Well, I think it looks good on you, falling over your face like that.
二科病院
"NISHINA HOSPITAL"
...CASES OF MEMORY LOSS ARE FAIRLY COMMON.
診察室
"EXAMINING ROOM"

WHEN THE ORIGINAL MEMORIES RETURN...
...THE SUBJECT FORGETS EVERYTHING THAT HAPPENED WHILE HE HAD AMNESIA.
IN YOUR CASE, YOU WERE IN A TRAFFIC ACCIDENT THAT CAUSED YOU TO LOSE YOUR MEMORY FOR TWO YEARS.
I'VE BEEN IN CHARGE OF YOUR CASE, AND YOU PROBABLY DON'T REMEMBER ME EITHER, RIGHT?
NO, SIR...
Sorry...
I THOUGHT THIS MIGHT HAPPEN, SO I ASKED YOU TO START UP A JOURNAL, JUST IN CASE.
DID YOU DO IT?
I DON'T KNOW!
OH-- NO, YOU WOULDN'T.
WELL, TRY LOOKING AROUND YOUR ROOM FOR IT.
IF YOU KEPT IT PROPERLY, THE JOURNAL SHOULD MAKE IT CLEAR WHOM YOU MET AND WHAT HAPPENED TO YOU OVER THE LAST TWO YEARS.
...YES, SIR...

FILLING IN A TWO-YEAR VOID IS GOING TO BE TOUGH...
...BUT HANG IN THERE.
科
TAKE CARE, NOW.
NOW, JUST A...
WHADDAYA MEAN, "TAKE CARE, NOW"?!
SIGH IT'S JUST TOO BAD.
UNH!?
FOR THE LAST TWO YEARS...
...YOU WERE SO QUIET, GENTLE AND POLITE...
Maybe because you didn't understand anything...
WHO THE HELL'RE YOU TALKIN' ABOUT?
OH, DEAR!
TIME TO GO TO MY PART-TIME JOB!
BE SURE TO HEAD STRAIGHT HOME ON YOUR OWN!
alone
ぽつん
Do you usually leave me like this?
When your own son's so full of anxiety?
SO IT ALL BOILS DOWN TO THAT, HUH?

MAYBE I'M THE ONE WHO GOT TAKEN OVER BY AN ALIEN...!
THE "ME" THAT I KNOW...
...IS 14 YEARS OLD, IN NINTH GRADE AND 5'5" TALL.
BUT THE CURRENT "ME"...
...IS 16 YEARS OLD, IN ELEVENTH GRADE AND IS ALMOST 5'8".
No wonder everything looks shorter...
WAIT A MINUTE...!! HOW THE HELL AM I SUPPOSED TO FILL THIS GAP...?!
EVEN IF I WENT TO SCHOOL, I WOULDN'T KNOW ANYBODY THERE.
WOULDN'T KNOW MY CLASSES EITHER, OF COURSE...
DAMN, I'M DEPRESSED ALREADY!

WELL, AS LONG AS I DIDN'T COMMIT ANY CRIMES, THAT'S SOMETHING, AT LEAST.
... ...
ERRT
CRIMES ...
....!
OH, GOD...
ZOOM
...YOU BETTER NOT HAVE USED MY BODY TO DO ANYTHING WEIRD!
OKAY, FIRST THAT JOURNAL ...
...THEN A HAIRCUT...
SQUEEE
....
GRAB
HOLD IT!!
?!
WHAT--?!

WHOA!
SCARY-LOOKIN' DUDE...
HEY...
...HOW COME YOU SKIPPED SCHOOL TODAY?
?!
DIDN'T YOU PROMISE TO COME BY MY PLACE ON THE WAY BACK TODAY?

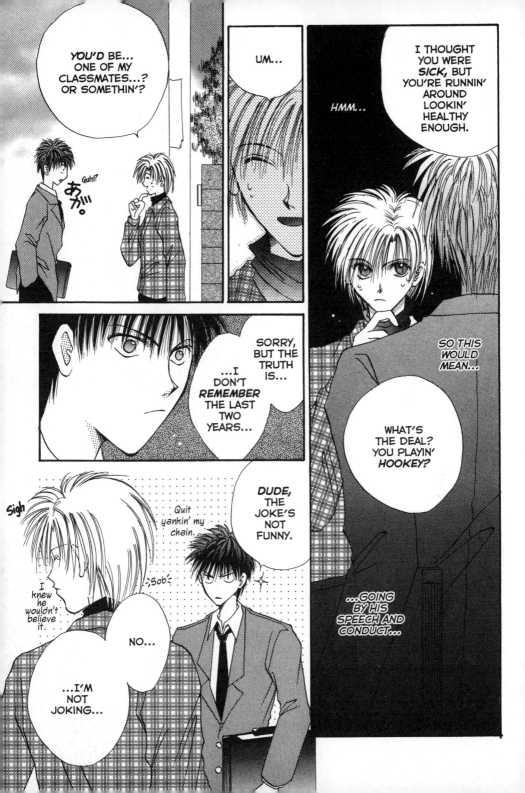

YOU'D BE... ONE OF MY CLASSMATES...? OR SOMETHIN'?

Guh!?

あが。

UM...

HMM...

I THOUGHT YOU WERE *SICK,* BUT YOU'RE RUNNIN' AROUND LOOKIN' HEALTHY ENOUGH.

SORRY, BUT THE TRUTH IS...

...I DON'T *REMEMBER* THE LAST TWO YEARS...

DUDE, THE JOKE'S NOT FUNNY.

SO THIS *WOULD* MEAN...

WHAT'S THE DEAL? YOU PLAYIN' *HOOKEY?*

Sigh

Quit yankin' my chain.

Sob

I knew he wouldn't believe it.

NO...

...I'M NOT JOKING...

...GOING BY HIS SPEECH AND CONDUCT...

IT'S THE *TRUTH.*
WHEN MY MEMORIES UP TO THE TRAFFIC ACCIDENT CAME BACK...
...I LOST ALL MY MEMORIES FROM *AFTER* THE ACCIDENT INSTEAD.
SO...
ちら...
Glance
I'M *SORRY,* BUT...
...I DON'T KNOW WHO YOU ARE.
WH-...
ANYWAY, I'M HEADIN' HOME TO HUNT UP MY JOURNAL.
SO, UH, I'LL CATCH YOU *LATER*...
ギィ
CREEAK
YOU... YOU *DON'T KNOW* WHO I *AM...?*

NO WAY...
WAIT!!
KSSH
?!
YOU'RE SAYING YOU'VE FORGOTTEN ME?!
WHA- ...
YOU'VE CALLED MY NAME WITH THAT SAME VOICE!! WITH THIS SAME MOUTH!!
WHERE'S THE HIROFUMI WHO SMILED AT ME UNTIL YESTERDAY?!!
WHERE'S ...?
DIDN'T YOU TELL ME...

...THAT YOU LOVED ME?!!!
Huh?!
Glomp
WHAT THE F...?
Wh-tsh
"LOVED"...?

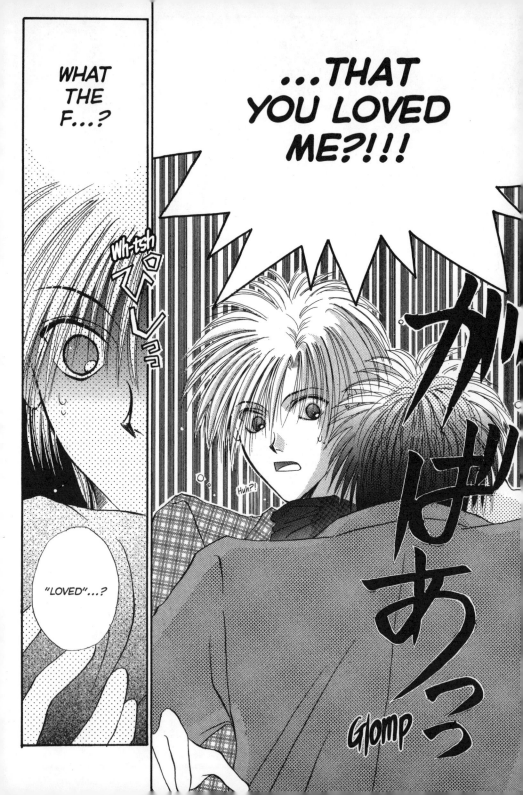

Grip
W-WHOA, NOW, WAIT A SEC...
I SAID...
...I LOVED...?
NOD
...LOVED YOU?
NOD
UH... HOO, BOY...
drip
drip
WAIT A SEC, HERE.
THAT WOULD MEAN THAT YOU AND I ARE...
sweat
of course!!
WE'RE LOVERS!!
DON'T SAY THAT!!!
I don't want to hear it!
NO WAY... I'VE BEEN GOING OUT WITH A GUY...!!
NGA NGA NGA NG
Oh, you screwed up big time, you damn alien...!!
Hmph!
GASP
OH, BUT...
WAIT!!

WE'RE TALKIN' PLATONIC LOVE, RIGHT?!
Since we're both guys and all?!
Right?
WELL, IN BASEBALL TERMS ...
...WE DID NINE INNINGS ALL 'ROUND THE BASES!!
GA-DUNNG
HIROFUMI ...?
UBER DEFEAT
OH, THIS IS WAY WORSE THAN A CRIME...
I NEVER THOUGHT I'D TURN INTO A HOMO ...!!
And I'm the bottom, too!?
THNGG
THNGG
THNGG
GAH!
MY LIFE IS OVER!
WAAAH!
GOING INSANE
Grrr!
What the hell!?
WHADDAYA MEAN, "OVER"?!
If you'd have just shut up and listened for a sec...

REMEMBER WHAT YOU TOLD ME, HIROFUMI!?
YOU SAID, "GENDER DOESN'T MATTER. I LOVE YOU AS A HUMAN BEING"!!
EUGH, WHAT A TYPICAL GAY LINE!
HIRO-FUMI!?
LOOK, I'M NOT INTO GOING OUT WITH GUYS!!
AND I'VE COMPLETELY FORGOTTEN WHO YOU ARE!!
NNNGH!
JUST FORGET ABOUT ME TOO!!
Okay?
I CAN'T!!
KRKKK
I LOVE YOU!
I REALLY LOVE YOU, HIROFUMI!!
HOW CAN I FORGET YOU WHEN YOU'RE RIGHT HERE IN FRONT OF ME?!

I LOVE YOUUU!!
mutter
Look, it's the Mizui boy.
WAH!
mutter mutter
I thought he was looking nice these days.
whisper whisper
YOU ...
YOU MORON!!
PANT PANT
CUT IT OUT!! THE NEIGHBORS'LL THINK IT'S A LOVERS' QUARREL!!
WELL, IT IS, AIN'T IT!?
I WON'T STOP UNTIL YOU REMEMBER ME, HIROFUMI!!
I LOVE YOU HIROFUMIIII!
.....
You... you sonofa ...
whisper
mutter mutter
OKAY, FINE, GET INSIDE!!
GOT TOO MANY PEOPLE STARIN' OUT HERE!!
I knew it!
WHISPER
GOSSIP
See, it has to be!
Squee
MMNGH...
THANK YOU VERY MUCH!

OKAY, FOR NOW...
...I'LL GO GET YOU SOMETHING TO DRINK.
I'LL LISTEN TO YOU AFTER THAT.
JUST PICK A GOOD SPOT TO SIT AND WAIT.
....
OH-- BETTER FIND THAT ALIEN'S JOURNAL FIRST...
カチャ
Ch-click
"CH-CLICK"?
VWIP
THE LOCK ...
JUST TELLING YOU WON'T DO ANY GOOD!!

AND SINCE TALK WON'T WORK...
...I'LL JUST ASK YOUR BODY!!!
LEAN
J-...
HUH....?
...JUST A GODDAMN MINUTE!!
HEY!! HOLD IT!! CALM DOWN!!
Just tell me and I'll get it, I swear!!
SHUT UP!
I already told you and you didn't!!
THMP CRASH
UNH--!
thupf

EVEN IF YOUR BRAIN DOESN'T REMEMBER, YOUR BODY SHOULD, RIGHT?!
YOU HEAR ME?!
'CAUSE I KNOW EVERYTHING ABOUT YOUR BODY!!
GRRRK
D-... DAMMIT!
NO FAIR-- HE'S MUCH HEAVIER!
RE-MEMBER ME!
!!
HIS NOSE...
WHA...?
SHUDDER
WH-... WHAT'S GOING ON?!
M-MY STRENGTH IS FADING...

S- ... STOP IT!!
THIS... DOES NOT LOOK GOOD...!!
WHOA ... JUST A...
I WILL NOT STOP IT!!
shff
OOH...
JERK
--?!
Yikes!
MY VOICE JUST... I DIDN'T MEAN TO...!!
What the hell was that "ooh" just now?!
HE... HE REALLY DOES KNOW MY BODY...
L- ... LEMME GO!!
thup

NEVER !!
!!
WHAT'LL I DO? I DON'T HAVE THE STRENGTH...
IF THIS KEEPS UP, I...
....KNH!
S-...

STOP IT, PLEASE!! I'M BEGGING YOU!!
TWITCH
!!
YOU'RE GOING TO CRY...
!
YOU DON'T LIKE ME ...?

BA-BUMP
YOU... REALLY HATE ME...
...THAT MUCH NOW...?!!
UH, I...

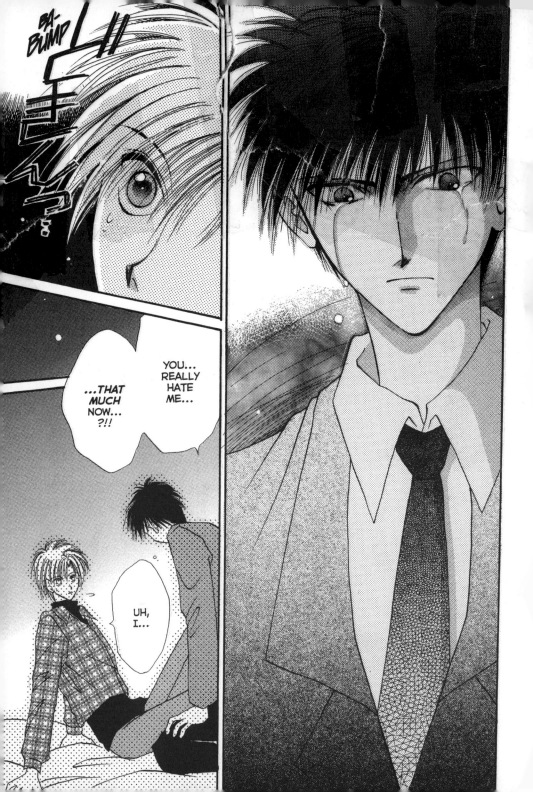

FINE, THAT DOES IT!!
YOU ARE NOT HIROFUMI!!
SHOOM
W-... WAIT...
SLAM
....
WHAT...
WHAT THE HELL?!!
LATER, TAKA-GISHI.
YO.
CREEE
キィ
ばん
BAM
JUMP
AAAH!
...DAIGO?!
ZOOM
WAAAAH!
わーんっ

ガチャ
ch-clak
HIRO-FUMI?!
DAIGO JUST FLEW OUT OF HERE, BAWLING...
ぎょ
ULP
...NF.
Whoa... he's crying too!
...WHAT HAPPENED?
D-... DID YOU HAVE A FIGHT?
WHY!?
I WAS THE VICTIM HERE!!
SO WHY IS IT... ?!!

WHY WAS HE LOOKING AT ME THAT WAY...?!!
LIKE... LIKE SOME LITTLE, ABANDONED ANIMAL...!!
WHAT THE HELL...
IT'S LIKE *I'M* THE BAD GUY HERE ...!!
ずきん...
throb
MY CHEST HURTS!
oh!
WHY DO I FEEL LIKE THIS FOR SOME JERK I DON'T EVEN *KNOW*!
Sniff Sniff
AH!
THAT'S RIGHT!
WAIT RIGHT THERE!
ガチャッ
KCHAK
CHIKA?!

HERE.
A LETTER ...?
WHO FROM ...?
FROM THE OLD YOU.
SORRY, YOU TOLD ME TO GIVE IT TO YOU WHEN YOUR MEMORY CAME BACK.
HEY!
OH, YOU ALSO SAID THE JOURNAL'S HIDDEN, SO FEEL FREE TO SEARCH FOR IT.
BASTARD.
That really pisses me off!

A LETTER FROM THE ALIEN WHO LIVED USING MY BODY FOR TWO YEARS...

flaf

thmp-thmp

Dear Myself

DEAR...

...MYSELF...

...AND...

"FINALLY..."

THE LETTER TO "MYSELF" WAS ALL ABOUT...

...THE EVENTS OF MY TWO MISSING YEARS...

"THERE'S SOMEONE I LOVE."

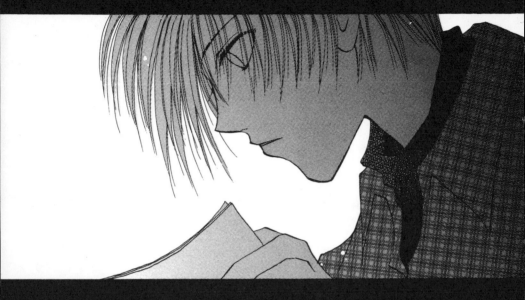

"MY GREATEST WORRY IS WHAT WILL BECOME OF THAT PERSON WHEN I'M GONE."

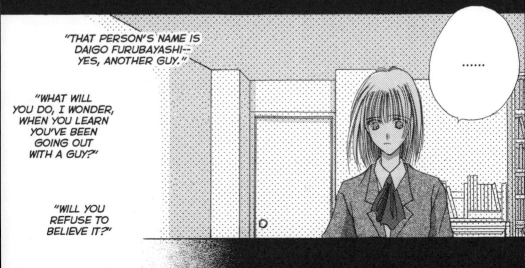

"THAT PERSON'S NAME IS DAIGO FURUBAYASHI-- YES, ANOTHER GUY."

"WHAT WILL YOU DO, I WONDER, WHEN YOU LEARN YOU'VE BEEN GOING OUT WITH A GUY?"

"WILL YOU REFUSE TO BELIEVE IT?"

......

"BUT I BEG YOU, PLEASE DON'T LEAVE HIM ALONE..."
"...BECAUSE WHILE HE SEEMS SCARY AND TOUGH AT FIRST GLANCE, HE'S REALLY VERY LONELY."
"MY HEART ACHES WHEN I SEE HIS MISERABLE EYES..."
"...AND I LOVE TO SEE HIS SMILE. SO, I WANT HIM ALWAYS TO BE SMILING."
"DON'T YOU AGREE?"
"I'M SURE YOU DO."
"AFTER ALL..."

"...YOU..."
"...ARE ME!"
CRITCH
--NNGRR.
LIKE HELL ...!!
YOU ARE NOT ME...!!
I MEAN...

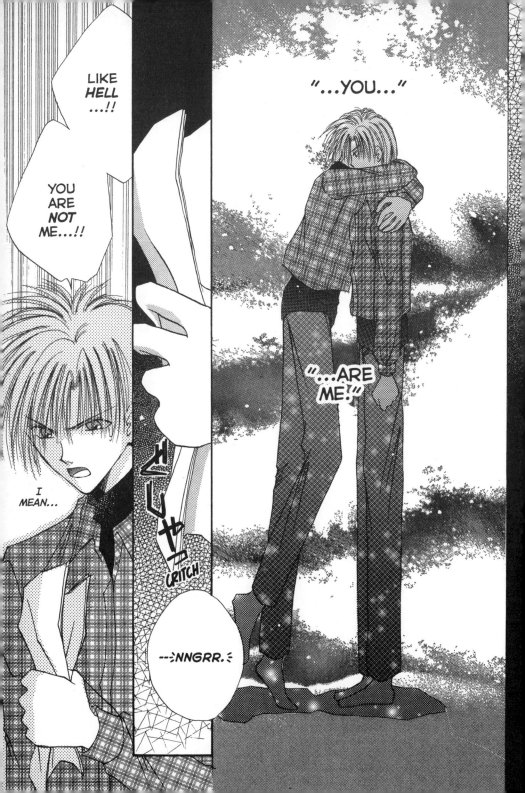

...I DON'T KNOW NOTHIN' ABOUT THOSE FEELINGS.
I DON'T KNOW NOTHIN' ABOUT HIM.
I DON'T RE-CALL ANY OF THIS--
THROB
NNGH...
--BUT...

...IF THAT'S SO...
...THEN WHAT'S THIS PAIN IN MY CHEST...?
LISTEN...
HIROFUMI...
YOU ALWAYS TOLD ME...
"HE'S SO LONELY, I CAN'T LEAVE HIM BE."
!
YOU AND DAIGO...
...WERE SO CLOSE...
Yeah, better not say they were all over each other.
...AND YET YOU'RE GONNA DUMP HIM?
COULD YOU LIVE WITH THAT?
-- ...

ずきん… Throb
THIS PAIN IN MY HEART…
…WAS BORN WITHIN ME…
…BECAUSE MY BODY…
…REMEM-BERED HIM.
GRSH
I GUESS…
…I'LL JUST HAVE TO ACCEPT IT.

IT WASN'T AN ALIEN...
...LIVING INSIDE ME...
...IT WAS MYSELF.
AFTER ALL, YOU ARE ME.
--...

SAY, CHIKA...
YOU, UH...
YOU KNOW HOW TO... CONTACT HIM?
!
UH-HUH!!
WAIT JUST A SEC!!
どたどたどた
thff thff thff
...
...
...
HO, BOY...
OH, WELL...
シャッ
shufft
...GUESS IT CAN'T BE HELPED.

I DIDN'T PLAN TO BECOME GAY...
...BUT IF MY HEART'S GONNA PAIN ME LIKE THIS...
WOW... NICE DAY OUT.
...WHAT ELSE CAN I DO?
FLAFF
WELL, FOR NOW...
...I GUESS I SHOULD START BY SEEING HIS SMILE.

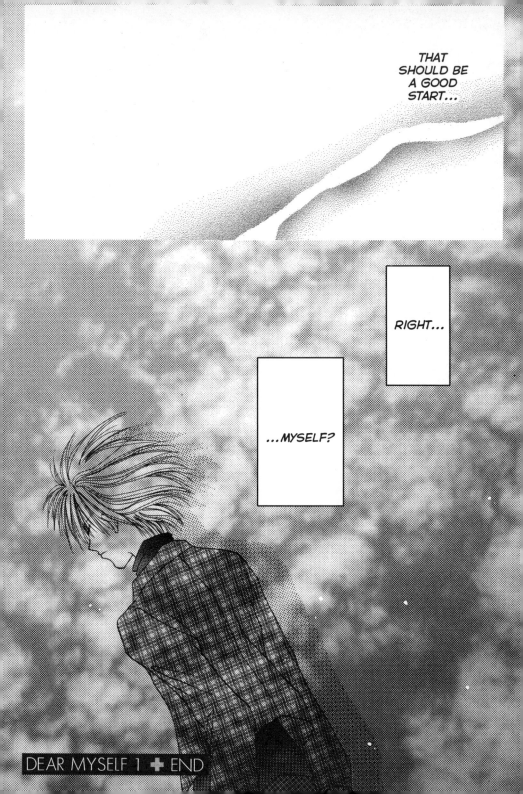

THAT
SHOULD BE
A GOOD
START...

RIGHT...

...MYSELF?

DEAR MYSELF 1 ✚ END

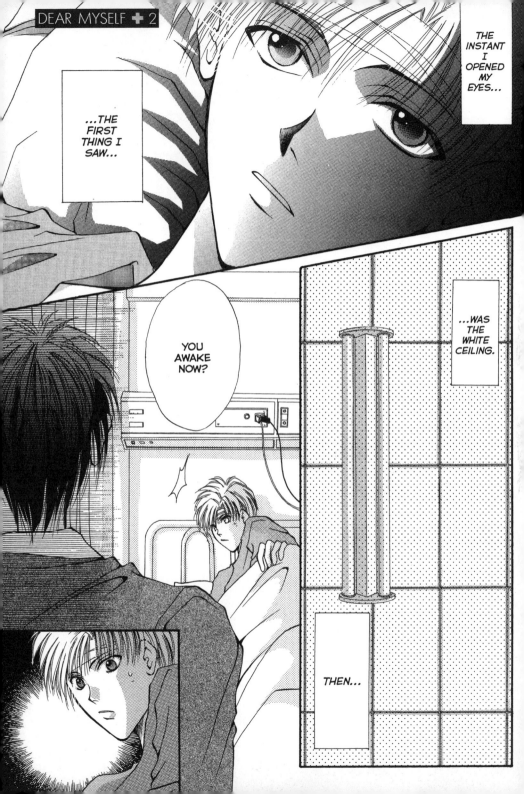

DEAR MYSELF ✚ 2

THE INSTANT I OPENED MY EYES...

...THE FIRST THING I SAW...

...WAS THE WHITE CEILING.

YOU AWAKE NOW?

THEN...

...THE NEXT THING I SAW...
...WAS A YOUNG BOY ON THE VERGE OF TEARS.
DEAR MYSELF, 2
ディア・マイセルフ

DAIGO, I...
...I CAN'T...
...TAKE ANY MORE.
I'M TIRED...
PLEASE...
...JUST LEMME SLEEP...
FORGET IT, HIROFUMI...
...WE'VE STILL GOT A *LONG* NIGHT AHEAD.
BUT...

...IF YOU'RE THAT TIRED, YOU CAN SLEEP WITH M--
POK
I SAID I'D BOOT YA UT IF YA KEPT SPOUTIN' OFF WEIRD STUFF LIKE THAT!!
KNOCK IT OFF, BOTH OF YOU!!
数学I MATH 1
E HAVEN'T MADE ANY ROGRESS!!
It's just been you two yakkin' away!
JUST WHY DO YOU THINK WE'RE HAVING THIS STUDY GROUP!?
WE'VE ALL GOT TESTS COMING UP!!
ULP...
Sniff
AW, C'MON ...
IF I'M TIRED, I'M TIRED!
OH, BIG DEAL!!
Glp

NOT ONLY HAV YOU GON BACK TO BEING A FRESHMA ...!
IF YOU HAVE TO REPEAT ANOTHER YEAR...
...YOU'LL BE A GRADE BELOW US!
URK!
...I'LL KEEP AT IT...
Chika's harsh...
THAT'S RIGHT. SINCE THEN...
RIGHT, LET'S DO IT!!
They're freshmen to begin with.
...I COULDN'T REMEMBER ANYTHING SINCE 9TH GRADE...
...SO OF COURSE, THERE WAS NO WAY I COULD HANDLE 11TH-GRADE CLASSES...
LUCKY ME, I HAD TO START OVER FROM 10TH GRADE.
AND ON TOP OF THAT...
Nngh...
MAN, I DON'T GET THIS PROBLEM AT ALL!
WHICH ONE?
FWFF

HI...
HIRO-FUMIII!
I LOVE YOUUU!
Glomp
GAH!!
AAUGH!!
Crunch
ARRGH! QUIT GRABBIN' ME!!
FBRASH
......
AAAH!
...I STILL CAN'T CUT TIES WITH THIS GUY...
I TOLD YOU ALREADY!!
THE INSTANT YOU ACT LIKE MORE THAN A "FRIEND," WE'RE THROUGH!!
HUH? WAS THAT MORE THAN LIKE A FRIEND?
I've had enough.
ch-klik

AND IT'S ALL BECAUSE...
I CAN'T TAKE IT ANY MORE!
YOU AND I ARE NOW...
!!
SOB
...OF THIS PAIN IN MY HEART!!
UNGH!
THROB
whine
DON'T CRY... I WON'T GET MAD AGAIN...
stagger
THANKS TO THIS PESKY PARTING GIFT FROM WHEN I HAD AMNESIA...
...I CAN'T DO SQUAT-ALL AGAINST HIS TEARS...
THROB
THROB
THROB
Wag Wag
Really? Really?

Grrr...
I EVEN GAVE UP CUTTING THIS OVERGROWN MOP JUST TO SHUT OFF HIS FAUCET...
BUT I THINK IT LOOKS GOOD ON YOUUU!
...
THROB THROB
DAMMIT...
WHY THE HELL DOES MY CHEST HAVE TO HURT SO MUCH?!!
HMPH-- I STILL AIN'T FOUND THAT JOURNAL YET.
WHERE THE HELL DID MY OLD SELF HIDE IT?!!
This still leaves me all in the dark!
JOURNAL?
thp
shff
IF YOU'RE TALKING ABOUT YOUR JOURNAL, I'VE GOT IT.
!!
Here.

WH-WHAT ARE YOU DOING WITH THAT?!
DIDN'T YOU TELL ME?
"I'M TRUSTING YOU WITH THIS, SO BRING IT TO SCHOOL EVERY DAY."
DAMN ME... I SET IT UP SO I'D NEVER HAVE FOUND THIS IF I'D SPLIT UP WITH HIM...
Grumble...
HEY, HIRO-FUMI...
WHAT ABOUT STUDYING-ING?
BREAK TIME.
SKRRT
I'VE GOT A RIGHT TO KNOW ABOUT THOSE TWO YEARS!!
LET'S SEE.. THE FIRST ENTRY...
FLAP
THIS IT...?

THE INSTANT I OPENED MY EYES...
...THE FIRST THING I SAW...
...WAS THE WHITE CEILING.
THEN THE NEXT THING I SAW...
......
WHO ARE YOU...?

......
...WAS A YOUNG BOY...
...ON THE VERGE OF TEARS.
UMM...
WHY...?
THMP
THMP
どきん
WHY IS HE LOOKING AT ME LIKE THAT...?
ARE YOU...
TAK TAK TAK
カッカッカッ

shff
すっ…
UH...
WAIT..
WELL!
LOOKS LIKE WE'RE AWAKE!
!
AAH... HE'S LEAVING...!!
YOU'VE BEEN THROUGH QUITE A LOT.
YOU WERE BROUGHT HERE AFTER BEING IN A CAR ACCIDENT.
UM... EXCUSE ME...
YES?
THAT BOY...
...WHO LEFT JUST NOW...
OH, HIM. HIS NAME'S DAIGO.
HE SAVED YOUR LIFE BY DRAGGING YOU HERE.
HUH...?

DON'T WORRY.
HE'S HERE AS A PATIENT, SO YOU'LL SEE HIM AGAIN.
FIRST THINGS FIRST...
...LET'S WORRY ABOUT YOU.
THANK-FULLY, YOUR WOUNDS WERE LIGHT.
BUT YOU HAVE NOTHING WE COULD USE TO IDENTIFY YOU.
WE'D LIKE TO CONTACT YOUR FAMILY.
COULD YOU TELL ME ABOUT YOURSELF?
--YES, SIR...
LET'S SEE, I'M...
...WHAT THE...?

HUH?
WHA? THAT'S WEIRD...
... ...
MY MIND'S A BLANK!
WHAT'S WRONG?
UM...I'D LIKE TO ASK YOU SOMETHING, IF I COULD...
YES?
WOULD YOU HAPPEN TO KNOW MY NAME?
......
That's what I'm asking YOU right now...
Silence
AMNESIA, EH?

IN THAT CASE, WE'LL HAVE TO WAIT UNTIL YOUR FAMILY PUTS IN A SEARCH REQUEST.
NOW, JUST A MINUTE...
WE'LL KEEP YOU HERE 'TIL THEN.
WELL, TAKE CARE.
ぱたん
Pchnk
...IS THIS FOR REAL...?
I FEEL LIKE...
...I'M SHIP-WRECKED IN THE MIDDLE OF A HUGE OCEAN...
UGH... NASTY. MY MIND REALLY IS BLANK...
LET'S SEE... WHAT CAN I REMEMBER...
I'D LIKE TO SEE HIM AGAIN...
THINKING ABOUT IT...

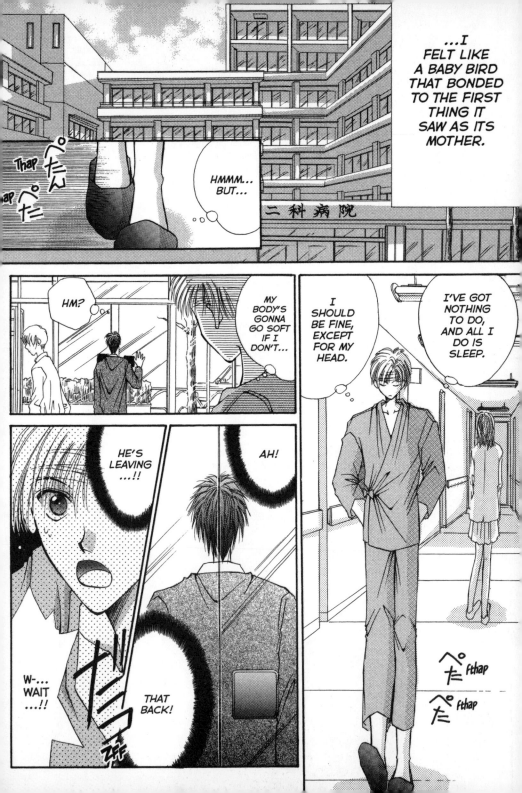

...I FELT LIKE A BABY BIRD THAT BONDED TO THE FIRST THING IT SAW AS ITS MOTHER.

ぺた
Thap
ぺた
Thap

HMMM... BUT...

二科病院

HM?

MY BODY'S GONNA GO SOFT IF I DON'T...

I SHOULD BE FINE, EXCEPT FOR MY HEAD.

I'VE GOT NOTHING TO DO, AND ALL I DO IS SLEEP.

HE'S LEAVING ...!!

AH!

THAT BACK!

W-... WAIT ...!!

ぺた fthap
ぺた fthap

Blink
ぱっ
OKAY!!
HEY, YOU...
I'LL CATCH HIM AT THE LIGHT!!
ZOOM
WHAT?!!
WAIT... IT'S STILL RED?!
BRRRMM...
AND THERE'S LOADS OF TRAFFIC ...!!

HONK
HOOONK
IS HE TRYIN' TO GET KILLED?!
WH-...
WHOA, STUPID!
WHAT THE HELL ARE YOU DOING? DAIGO!!
ZOOM

...!!
YOU...
GET OUT OF THE STREET!!
WHOA...!
Whump

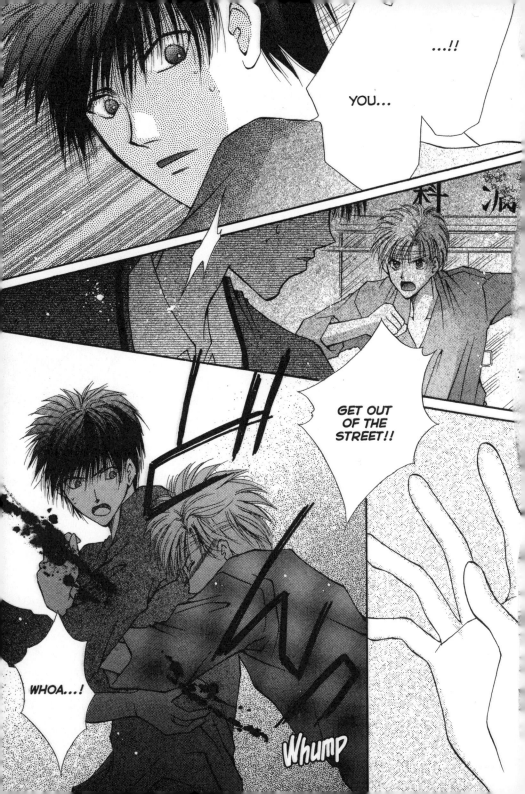

THAK
Are... are you okay!?
BRRMMM
......
OWW...
WOW, THAT WAS CLOSE!!
RIGHT?
AAAAH! WAKE UUUP!!
Don't diiie!
RATTLE RATTLE
だら
SLUMP

"EXAMINING ROOM"
OH, HE'LL BE FINE.
IT'S NOT THAT SERIOUS.
診察
JUST LET HIM BE FOR A BIT AND HE'LL COME AROUND.
WELL, WHO'D HAVE THOUGHT-- THIS TIME YOU DRAGGED IN *DAIGO!*
Ha Ha Ha!
UH, THAT ASIDE, DOCTOR...
HE...
HE LOOKED LIKE HE STEPPED OUT INTO TRAFFIC ON PURPOSE...
AAH, RIGHT...
...I SEE...

I'D HOPED HE'D BE BETTER BY NOW.
BETTER ...?
Stare
......
HMM...
THIS IS JUST BETWEEN US, ALL RIGHT?
HE'S HAD SOMETHING OF A CHECKERED PAST...
EVEN NOW, HE'S GETTING PSYCHIATRIC COUNSELING.
!
FROM THE LOOK OF IT...
...HE WAS ABANDONED BY SOMEONE CLOSE TO HIM AND NOW THINKS NOBODY WANTS HIM...
SO SOMETIMES... HE DOES THINGS LIKE THAT.

ABANDONED...?
"THIS GUY WAS ABANDONED IN THE STREET."
"I JUST FOUND HIM."
HE DIDN'T LET GO OF YOU EASILY.
HE FINALLY PULLED AWAY FROM YOU AFTER A NUMBER OF REQUESTS, BUT...
...HE WOULD NEVER LEAVE YOUR SIDE.
EVEN WHEN HE DRAGGED YOU IN HERE, HE SAID...
I WONDER IF THIS INSTANCE WAS DUE TO THAT...

...OH...!!
IS THAT WHY!?
IS THAT WHY HE WAS....
LOOKING AT ME THAT WAY...?
WELL, I'VE GOT A MEETING TO GO TO...
YOU SHOULD GET BACK TO YOUR ROOM.
PTAM
...YES, SIR...
......
THNK
oh!
!

YOU'RE...
...AWAKE NOW?
......
THANKS FOR...
...BUTTING IN...
GRR!
WHADDA' MEAN, "BUTTIN IN"?!!
JUST THAT-- BUTTING IN!!
YOU GOT IN MY WAY!!
OF COURSE I DID!! YOU WERE ABOUT TO GET KILLED!!
THAT'S RIGHT! SO WHAT?!!

WHO CARES IF I DIE?!!
NOBODY NEEDS ME ANYWAY...!!
IT'S GOT NOTHIN' TO DO WITH YOU, SO BUTT OUT!!
LIKE HELL IT'S GOT NOTHING TO DO WITH ME!!
PAKK
ばき…
UNH...
がらがっしゃーん
KRUNGRSH

WHAT THE HELL...
SNAG
YOU!!
YOU BROUGHT ME IN, RIGHT?!
...WHAT...
LOOK!!
IF YOU WERE GONE, I'D BE SUNK!!
WAIT A MINUTE...
YOU'RE THE ONLY PERSON I KNOW RIGHT NOW!!
YOU BROUGHT ME IN, SO YOU ACT RESPONSIBLE FOR ME!!
WHY AM I SPOUTING ALL THIS SELF-CENTERED STUFF...?
YOU DON'T JUST TRY TO GET YOURSELF OFFED!!

...BUT ...
...I DON'T CARE IF IT IS SELF-CENTERED...
throb
SO...
...DON'T LOOK AT ME LIKE THAT...
I WANTED TO SHOW HIM...
..."YOU'RE NOT UNWANTED"...
......
YOU...
...BELONG TO ME...?
IF YOU PUT IT THAT WAY...
...I BROUGHT YOU IN TOO, DAIGO...
...SO YOU BELONG TO ME.

YOU BELONG TO ME...
...AND I BELONG TO YOU?
YEP...
......
I SEE...
THAT'S WHEN...
HE SMILED ...!!
...I MET ANOTHER CAST-AWAY...

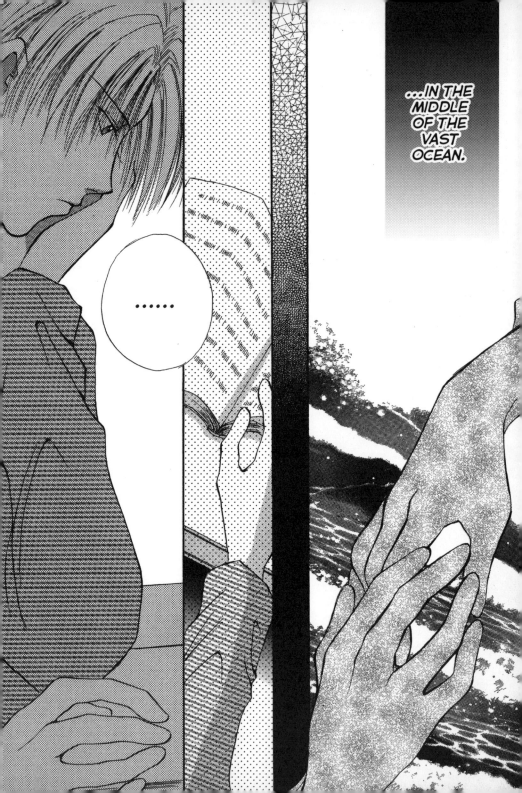

......

...IN THE
MIDDLE
OF THE
VAST
OCEAN.

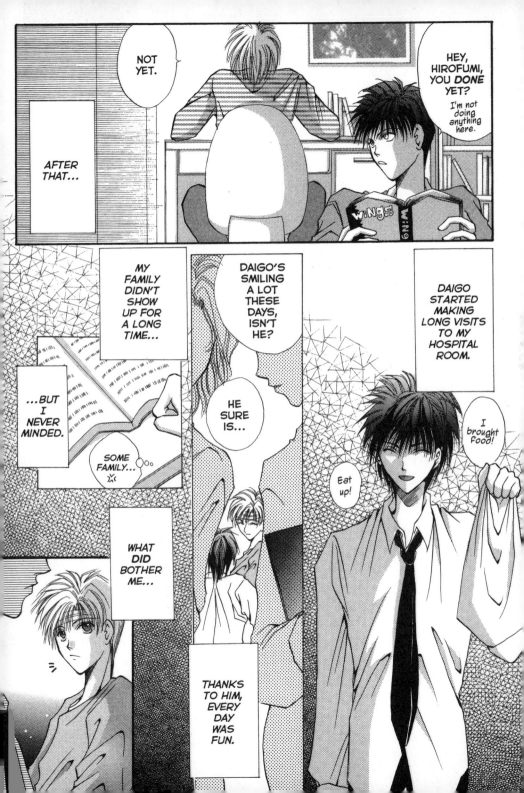

NOT YET.

AFTER THAT...

HEY, HIROFUMI, YOU *DONE* YET?

I'm not doing anything here.

MY FAMILY DIDN'T SHOW UP FOR A LONG TIME...

...BUT I NEVER MINDED.

SOME FAMILY... ノ;)く

WHAT DID BOTHER ME...

DAIGO'S SMILING A LOT THESE DAYS, ISN'T HE?

HE SURE IS...

THANKS TO HIM, EVERY DAY WAS FUN.

DAIGO STARTED MAKING LONG VISITS TO MY HOSPITAL ROOM.

I brought food!

Eat up!

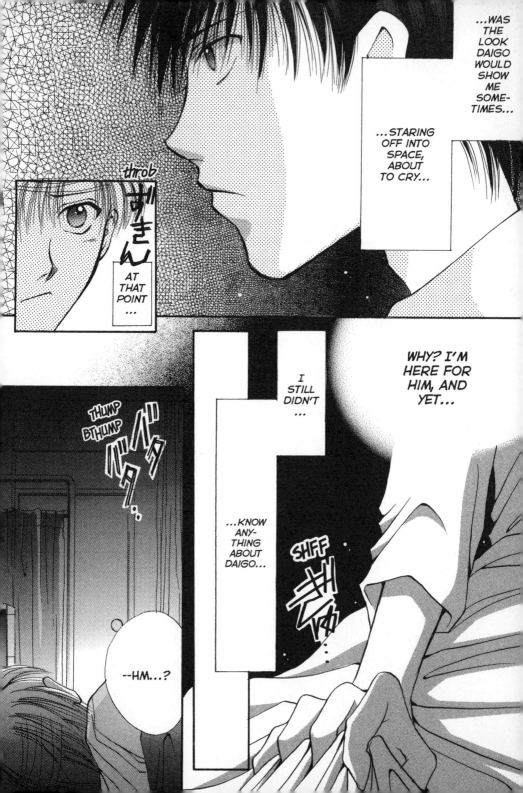

...WAS THE LOOK DAIGO WOULD SHOW ME SOMETIMES...

...STARING OFF INTO SPACE, ABOUT TO CRY...

throb

AT THAT POINT...

WHY? I'M HERE FOR HIM, AND YET...

THUMP BTHUMP

I STILL DIDN'T...

...KNOW ANYTHING ABOUT DAIGO...

SHFF

--HM...?

Hold it...!
WHAT'S GOING ON AT THIS HOUR...?
KRUNK
THUMP
CH-KLAK
JUMP
KCHAK
KCHAK
SLAM
WH-... WHO'S...
!
DAIGO...!?

WHAT'S THE PROBLEM...?!
WHY'D YOU COME HERE DRESSED LIKE THAT?!
DAIGO!!
OPEN THIS DOOR!
ガチャガチャッ
GCHAK GCHAK
DAIGO...?!
I HAD...
...A BAD DREAM...
WHAT...?
I DREAMED YOU WENT AWAY, JUST LIKE AKIHIKO...
AKIHIKO...?!
ARE YOU GONNA LEAVE ME TOO, AFTER ALL...?!

IS SOMETHING.. WEIRD ABOUT DAIGO...?
WH-... WHAT ARE YOU TALKING ABOUT?
I'M NOT GONNA GO OFF AND LEAVE YOU HERE...
......
DO YOU... LOVE ME...?
HUH...?
LOVE YOU?
UH... SURE...
I LIKE YOU A LOT, DAIGO, BUT...
ALL RIGHT, THEN...

...PROVE IT TO ME.
PROVE YOU LOVE ME.
PROVE... IT...?
BM-BMP

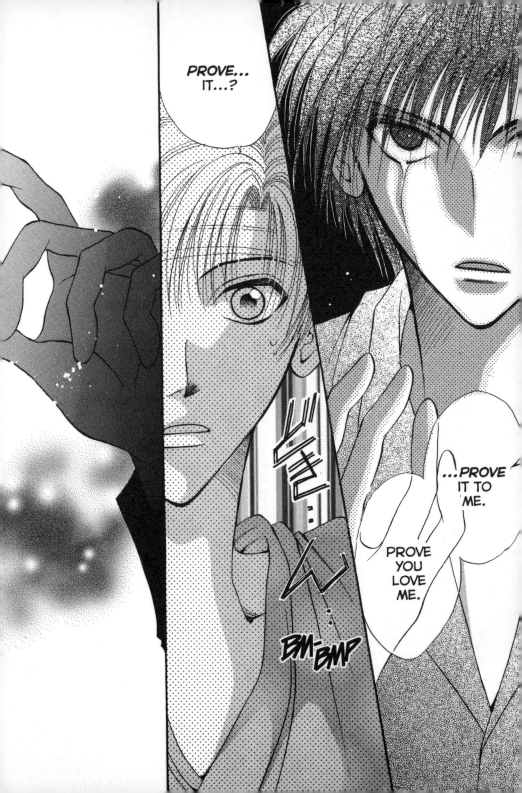

?!
THWA
GIVE YOUR-SELF...
...TO ME...!!
D-...
DAIGO...?!

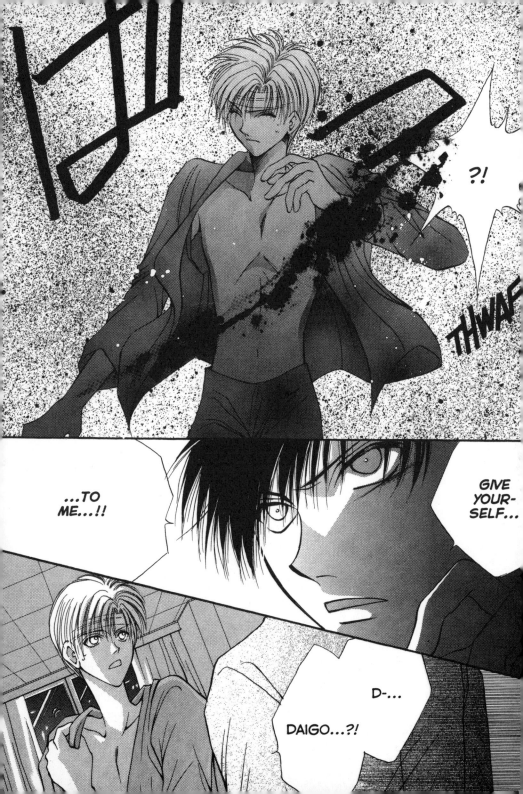

?!
KRAYASH
DOCTOR...!! THAT SOUND JUST NOW...
YOU!!
GO GET A KEY!! STAT!!
WHOA... HEY!
DAIGO...!!
TH-BMP
I SAID CUT IT OUT...!!
KRRNK

I'M A GUY!!
HEY...!!
GRIP
STOP IT!!
!!
THOK

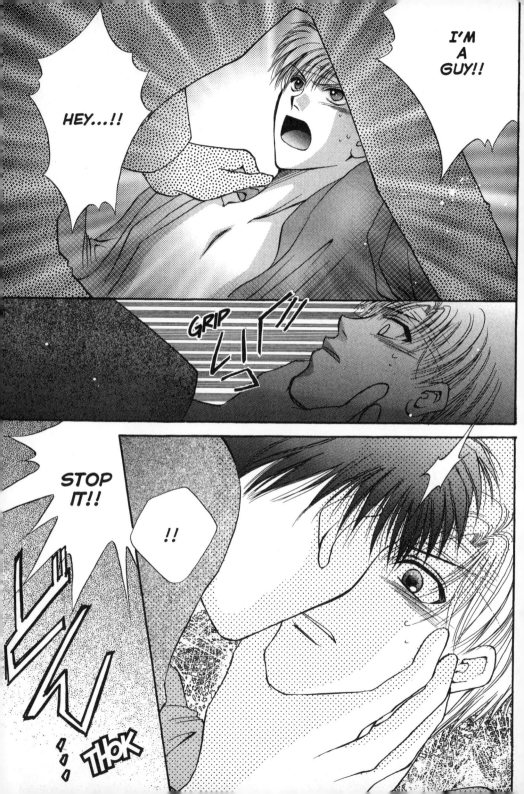

......
DAIGO...?
......
AKIHIKO...
HUH...?
WHERE DID YOU GO...?
AKIHIKO...
TOTTER
...NO...
I DON'T WANNA BE ALONE ANY MORE...!!

IF YOU'RE GONNA ABANDON ME...
...YOU MIGHT AS WELL KILL ME RIGHT NOW...!!
BM-BMP
DAIGO--?
CAN'T HE TELL BETWEEN DREAM AND REALITY...?!
BAM BAM
OPEN UP!
DOC-TOR... THE KEY...
DON'T LEAVE ME ALONE!!
LOVE ME... LIKE YOU DID BEFORE!!

DAIGO!!
BTAM
ばん
DAIGO...!!

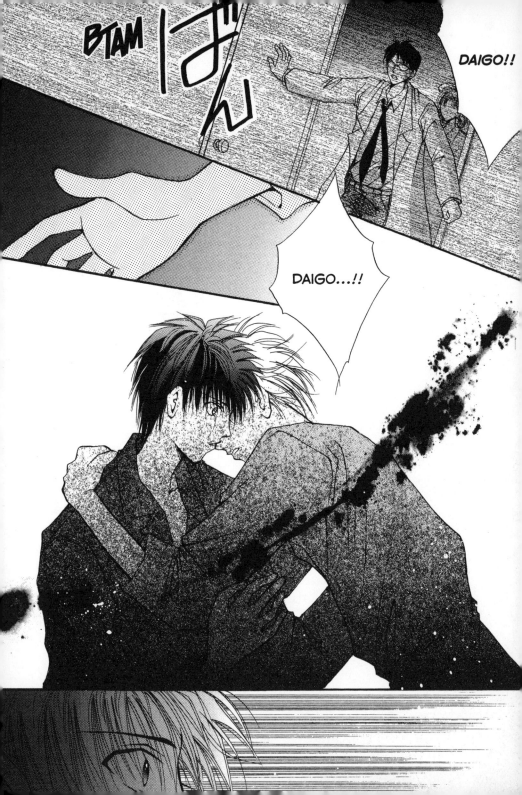

IT'S OKAY...
I'M RIGHT HERE...
"I'M RIGHT... HERE..."?
YOU WON'T GO AWAY...?
YOU WON'T LEAVE ME...?
THAT'S RIGHT. EASY, NOW...
I'LL BE RIGHT BY YOUR SIDE.

I'LL ALWAYS BE HERE FOR YOU.
SO...
...GET SOME REST NOW...
......
......
DAIGO...
LOOKS LIKE HE'S CALMED DOWN...

WHO MADE YOU CRY LIKE THIS?
IS HE... ALL RIGHT...?
"EXAMINING ROOM"
診察
YOU WERE SURPRISED, I'M SURE.
DAIGO'S BEEN KNOWN TO...
...DO THIS SORT OF THING FROM TIME TO TIME.
DOCTOR!!
JUST WHAT DID THIS "AKIHIKO"...
...HAVE TO DO WITH DAIGO?

HE WAS LIKE AN UNCLE TO DAIGO.
AND HE *ABANDONED* DAIGO?!
......
FIRST THINGS FIRST... I THINK...
...I THINK IT'S BETTER IF YOU... PULL AWAY FROM HIM.
?!
WHAT DO YOU MEAN?!
THAT'S...!!
RIGHT NOW, DAIGO IS STARTING TO OPEN HIMSELF UP TO YOU.
SO WHAT HAS THAT...

SUPPORTING DAIGO WILL BE TOO MUCH FOR YOU.
IF ANYTHING WENT WRONG THIS TIME, IT WOULD SURELY BE OVER FOR HIM....
RIGHT NOW, THERE'S STILL TIME TO--
I WOULD *NEVER* BETRAY DAIGO!!
NEVER...!!
BUT YOU MIGHT *FORGET* HIM.
WHAT...?!
WHEN AN AMNESIAC REGAINS HIS MEMORY, HE WILL OFTEN FORGET WHAT'S HAPPENED WHILE HE HAD AMNESIA.
AND EVEN IF YOU DON'T FORGET...
...WHEN YOUR FOURTEEN YEARS COME BACK TO YOU...
...I DON'T KNOW IF YOU'LL STILL NEED DAIGO LIKE YOU DO NOW.

BY THAT POINT, IT WILL BE TOO LATE...
...HIROFUMI MIZUI.
THAT NAME...
IS THAT MY...?
WE FOUND YOUR PARENTS.
IT SEEMS THEY HAPPENED TO BE ON VACATION.
THEY'LL BE CATCHING THE FIRST FLIGHT TOMORROW TO PICK YOU UP.
shrff
FORGET?!

ME, FORGET DAIGO?!
NO, I COULD NEVER--
カタ…
KLIK
はっ
Gasp
WHO'S THERE?!!
thap
DAIGO!!
ZWFF

DAIGO... WAIT!!
......
DAIGO!!
!!
DAIGO ...!!
SO, YOUR...
YOUR NAME'S HIROFUMI, HUH.

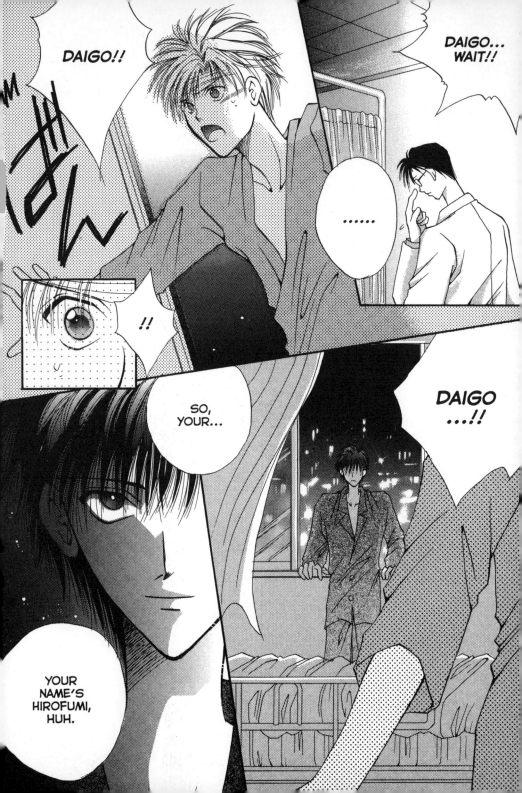

THAT'S GREAT.
DAI-...
SO YOU DON'T...
YOU'RE GOING HOME, RIGHT?
YOU'RE GOING SOMEWHERE FAR AWAY?
THEY'RE COMING TO GET YOU, RIGHT?
YOUR FAMILY, I MEAN.
...YOU DON'T NEED ME ANY MORE.

throb
I DON'T KNOW...
...WHEN MY MEMORIES WILL COME BACK...
--...
DAIGO...

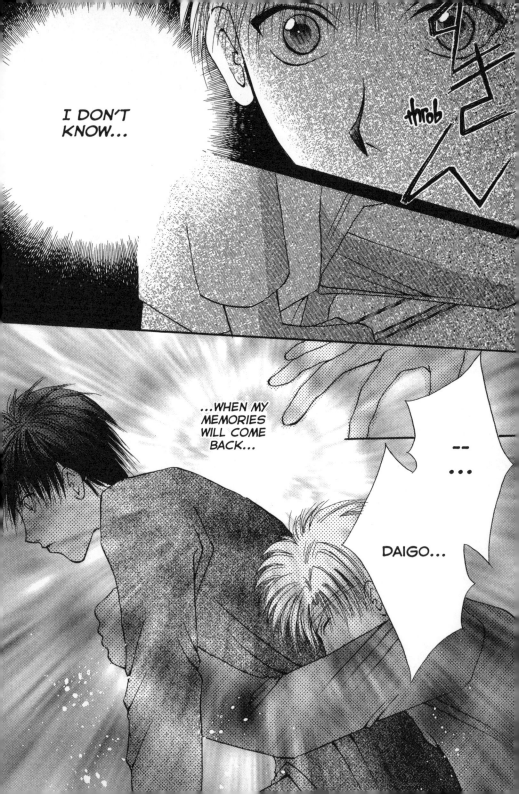

SO MY FAMILY'S COMING TO GET ME...
WE CAN STILL SEE EACH OTHER EASILY, RIGHT?!
I PROMISED YOU...
...I'D STAY BY YOUR SIDE, DIDN'T I?!!
I DON'T KNOW...
...IF I'LL FORGET YOU OR NOT...
HIROFUMI ...?
MORON!!
WHEN DID I SAY I WOULDN'T NEED YOU?!!

PROMISES...
I... I CAN'T TRUST PROMISES...
EVERYONE'S ALWAYS LIED TO ME...
ALL RIGHT...
...I'LL PROVE I'M TELLING THE TRUTH.
PROVE?

I'LL GIVE MYSELF TO YOU...
...COMPLETELY.
!!
HI-... HIROFUMI ..?
I MEAN... IT'S TRUE, RIGHT?
JUST LIKE I TOLD YOU...

...I BELONG TO YOU.
...BUT WHY SHOULD I HAVE TO ABANDON THIS BOY NOW...
...FOR THE SAKE OF SOME FUTURE I CAN'T EVEN PREDICT ...?
AKIHIKO ALSO TOLD ME...

..."I LOVE YOU" LIKE THAT.
I SEE...
DAIGO...
SO WHY...
...WHY DID HE ABANDON ME...?
ずきん
Throb
ARE THOSE EYES STILL SEARCHING FOR HIM...?

DAIGO ...
...LOOK AT ME...
JUST... AT... ME...
HIROFUMI...
...WHERE DOES IT HURT...?

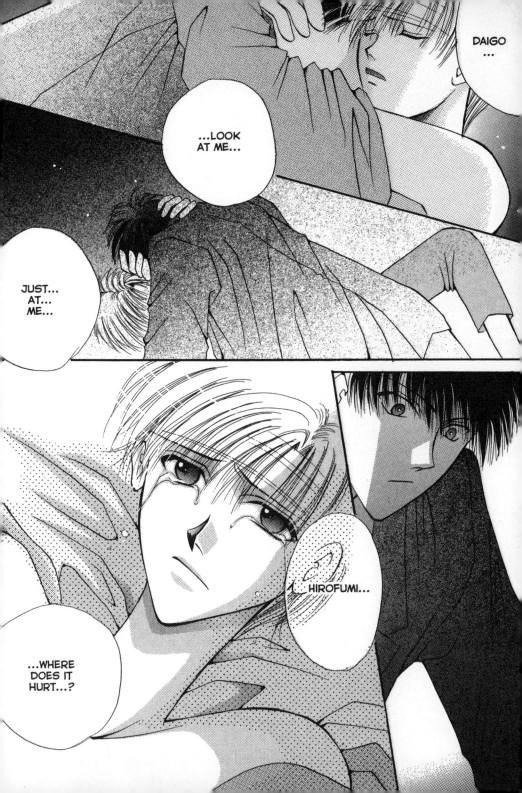

NO, IT'S NOT...
ARE YOU LONELY?
!
IT'S ALL RIGHT.
I'M HERE, AREN'T I?
......
HIROFUMI?

PLEASE, LORD...!!
I WANT TO BE BY HIS SIDE FOREVER.
I NEVER WANT MAKE HIM LOOK LIKE THAT AGAIN.
HIROFUMI ...?
I DON'T WANT TO FORGET.
I DON'T WANT TO FORGET.
YO, HIROFUMI...?
IF I COULD...

IF I COULD... JUST WATCH OVER HIS SMILE FOREVER...
--HIROFUMI.
HEY--!
HIROFUMIII!
WHAT THE... WHAT IS ALL THIS!..?
I DON'T KNOW ANYTHING ABOUT THIS, DO I...?
WE'RE OUT OF TIME FOR TONI-...
!
HIROFUMI-- *WHAT'S WRONG?!*
EH...?

HUH...?
THAT'S WEIRD. WHEN DID I START...
IT WON'T STOP.
HIROFUMI.
WHA...
!

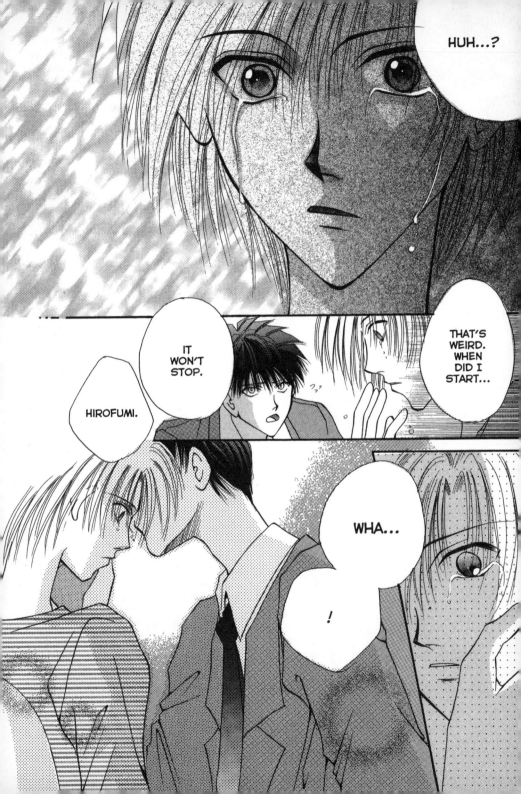

DON'T BE AFRAID.
I'M RIGHT HERE.
thmp thmp
DEAR MY-SELF...
I LOVE HIS SMILE.
SO, I WANT HIM ALWAYS TO BE SMILING.
DON'T YOU AGREE?

I'M SURE YOU AGREE, DON'T YOU?
STUPID...
YEAH, THAT'S RIGHT, MYSELF ...
I AGREE I DON'T HATE HIS SMILE...
Quit takin' advantage of my confusion to try strange crap...
BOOT
Meewww!
DEAR MYSELF 2 ✚ END

I'D BEEN WAITING FOR SO LONG...
...IN THIS DARK ROOM...
...FEELING OPPRESSED AND TEARFUL...
...SAD AND LONELY.
BUT WHEN I FELT I WAS ABOUT TO BE SWALLOWED UP IN THE BLACKNESS OF DESPAIR...
...YOUR HAND WAS HELD OUT TO ME...

DON'T CRY...
I'M RIGHT HERE...
DEAR MYSELF,3
ディア・マイセルフ

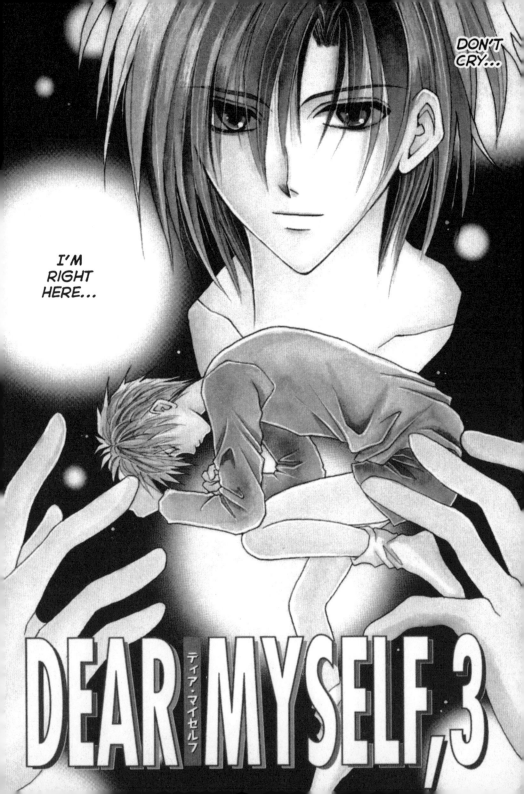

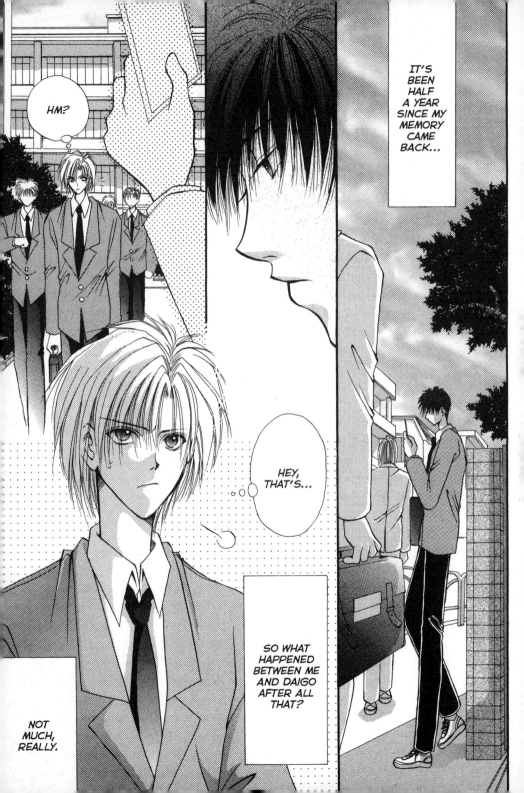

HM?

IT'S BEEN HALF A YEAR SINCE MY MEMORY CAME BACK...

HEY, THAT'S...

SO WHAT HAPPENED BETWEEN ME AND DAIGO AFTER ALL THAT?

NOT MUCH, REALLY.

DAIGO'S BEEN STICKING CLOSE AS A SHADOW, AS USUAL.
DAIGO!! WHAT THE HELL ARE YOU DOING THERE?!
JUMP
EVERY DAY, IT'S PURSUE AND RUN OFF.
HIROFUMI!!
shrff thff
I THOUGHT WE COULD GO HOME TOGETHER, SO I WAS LYING IN WAIT FOR YOU!!
NO WAY!
FORGET IT--NOT TODAY!!
Ga-Dungg
WHAAAT!?
TODAY'S MY FIRST FOLLOW-UP MEDICAL EXAMINATION IN A WHILE.
SEE YA
...BUT AS USUAL, I CAN'T JUST BRUSH HIM OFF.
NO! NO! I'M COMIN' WITH YOUUU!
thff
SO WE'VE PRETTY MUCH KEPT DRAGGING ON OUR RELATIONSHIP LIKE THIS.
throb throb
...DON'T CRY.
AND IT'S ALL BECAUSE I CAN'T STAND TO SEE HIM CRY.
Good grief.
LATELY, THOUGH ...

...I'VE BEEN THINKING ...
...ABOUT A LOT OF THINGS.
WELL, LONG TIME NO SEE, HIROFUMI!
HOW HAVE YOU BEEN FEELING SINCE THEN?
病院
PRESS
DO I *LOOK* ALL RIGHT TO YOU?
heh heh heh heh heh
...
VERY MUCH SO!!
Ha ha ha ha!
MEEEWWW!
YOU'RE A DOCTOR-- DO SOMETHING ABOUT THIS!! FOR THE PAST SEVERAL DAYS, HE'S BEEN CLINGIN' TO ME AND WON'T LET GO!
Lemme go, spaz!!
KRRRKK HRNNG
AH HA HA HA HA!
You're a lot wilder than I thought, Hirofumi!
FIRST, THOUGH, DOCTOR...

I FIGURED IT OUT FROM THE JOURNAL-- YOU *KNEW* ABOUT ME AND DAIGO, DIDN'T YOU?!
GRRR
Gotcha!
すきありっっ
SO WHY THE HELL DIDN'T YOU TELL ME WHEN I CAME HERE RIGHT AFTER MY MEMORIES CAME BACK?!!
ぎゅむっ
Glomp
... ...
YES... BUT THINK...
RRMBL RRMBL
IF I'D JUST BLURTED OUT, "OH, WHILE YOUR MEMORIES WERE GONE, YOU GOT ALL LOVEY-DOVEY WITH ANOTHER GUY"...
...IT WOULD'VE BEEN QUITE A SHOCK, RIGHT?
IT MIGHT'VE BEEN BETTER THAN SOME GUY LEANING ON ME OUT OF THE BLUE AND YELLING, "YOU AND I ARE LOVERS"!!
....
Um...
BUT IT'S SO NICE THAT YOU SEEM TO BE GETTING ALONG.
PLEASE DON'T CHANGE THE SUBJECT.

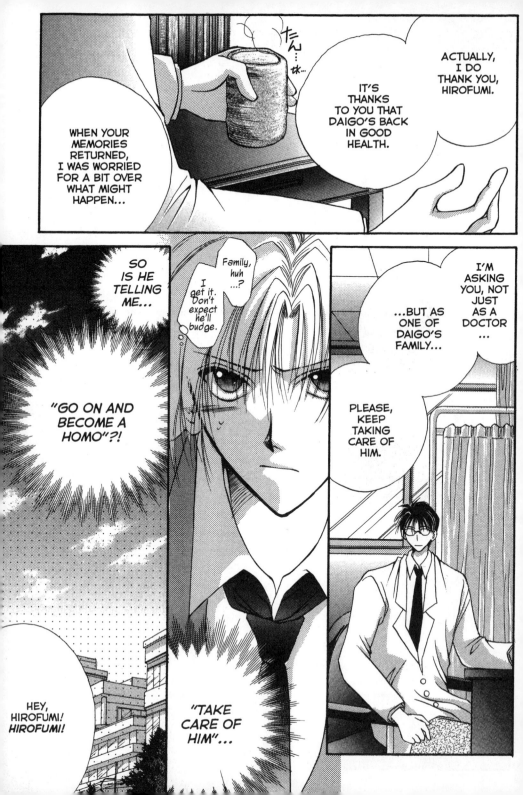

ACTUALLY,
I DO
THANK YOU,
HIROFUMI.

IT'S
THANKS
TO YOU THAT
DAIGO'S BACK
IN GOOD
HEALTH.

WHEN YOUR
MEMORIES
RETURNED,
I WAS WORRIED
FOR A BIT OVER
WHAT MIGHT
HAPPEN...

I'M
ASKING
YOU, NOT
JUST
AS A
DOCTOR
...

Family,
huh
...?

...BUT AS
ONE OF
DAIGO'S
FAMILY...

PLEASE,
KEEP
TAKING
CARE OF
HIM.

SO
IS HE
TELLING
ME...

I
get it.
Don't
expect
he'll
budge.

"GO ON AND
BECOME A
HOMO"?!

"TAKE
CARE OF
HIM"...

HEY,
HIROFUMI!
HIROFUMI!

WE GONNA GO STUDY OVER AT YOUR PLACE AGAIN TODAY?
......
...I HAVE TO WONDER...
... ...
Hey, Hirofumi!
You in there?
WHEN I LOOK CAREFULLY AT RECENT EVENTS...
...JUST HOW DO I FEEL ABOUT DAIGO...?

CLINGING AND WON'T LET GO, EH...?
COME TO THINK OF IT, IT *IS* ABOUT THAT TIME...
......
DAIGO...
I HOPE YOU'RE ALL RIGHT...
KNOCK IT OFF!!
KRASSSH
Yipe!

どす
thump
DAMMIT, DAIGO, LEGGO OF ME!!
HEY, WATCH THE HANDS!!
ばた
bump
どすん
thnk
ANOTHER HELPING, CHIKA?
Hee Hee Hee!
SURE-- JUST A SMALL ONE.
......
← DAD
LEMME GO!! GODDAMMIT, I SAID LET ME GO!
NO.
DON'T GIVE ME "NO"!
DIDN'T YOU COME HERE TO STUDY?!
rrrngrrrkkk
んぎぎぎぎ
MMNNFF...

...NO...!!
!!
TODAY I JUST... CAN'T TAKE IT ANY MORE!!
...WHAT THE HELL?!
USUALLY HE GIVES UP BY NOW...
WHUNNF
HEY...! WHOA...!
AACK!
SOMETHING'S REALLY WRONG WITH HIM TODAY!!

JUST-- ...
NO, DON'T-- ...
ULP!
MMMNN!
......
IT...IT FEELS SO GOOD...
I'M GOING ALL WEAK...

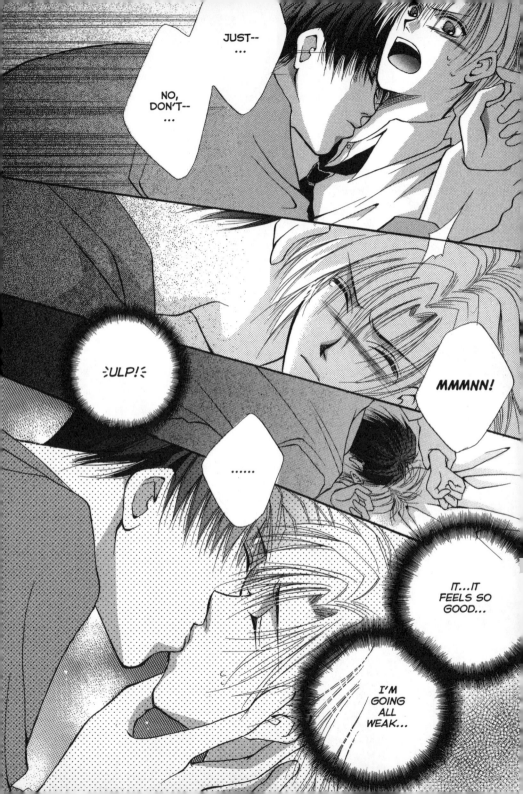

...OH YEAH, THAT'S RIGHT.
THIS GUY KNOWS ALL ABOUT MY BODY.
I GOTTA ADMIT, I WENT PALE READING ABOUT IT...
○○EMBER XX-- TODAY, DAIGO AND I TRIED ○x△□.
Eeeep! Don't write that sorta crap in your journal, you freak!
SO I GUESS ... IT CAN'T BE HELPED ...
HNN...
しん...
silence
WELL, IT CERTAINLY GOT QUIET.
oh!
MAYBE HE FINALLY GAVE IN?!
はっ
HUH
NO-- THIS IS NO TIME TO GET CARRIED AWAY!

GET OFF!
YEEK!
ばきーっ
KRAKK
DIDN'T I TELL YOU IF YOU TRIED ANYTHING FUNNY, WE'D BE THROUGH?!
HNNN... SNFF
WHADDAYA MEAN, "FUNNY"?
YOU KNOW I LOVE YOU!
SO WHY CAN'T I DO THAT?
hnn... snff
Throb
UNGH...
OKAY, IF YOU PUT IT THAT WAY, I'LL TELL YA...
I'VE HAD SOME REAL TRAUMAS WITH GAYS...
EVER SINCE I WAS LITTLE, THE LOCAL KIDS (BOYS, OF COURSE) WERE ALWAYS FALLING IN LOVE WITH ME.
CREEPY OLD PERVS WERE ALWAYS DOING UNSPEAKABLE THINGS TO ME.
I'd get love letters from my best friends, boys would give me chocolate and valentines, etc., etc....
whrrooo
......
哀愁
GRIEF

SO I VOWED IN MY HEART THAT I WOULD BECOME MORE *MANLY,* OR AT LEAST NEVER BECOME A *HOMO!* AND YET...
A guy loses his memory for a little bit, and look what happens!!
hngh SOB
WHAT THE *HELL?!*
WELL, IT'S TOO LATE TO PROTEST IT NOW!
YOU'VE GROWN UP SO PRETTY AND ALL!
THIS IS A MENTAL PROBLEM, YOU 'TARD! MENTAL!
Mentally, I'm still a virgin!
THKRASSH
YEEEE!
......
OKAY, THEN...

...SO WHAT DID YOU *MEAN* WHEN YOU SAID YOU'D STAY BY ME?
!!
すきん
Throb
...ULP!
WH-... WHAT DID I MEAN ...?
I'VE BEEN WANTING TO ASK YOU THAT FOR A WHILE NOW.

AGAIN...
THERE'S THAT LOOK AGAIN...
HIROFUMI...
...JUST HOW DO YOU FEEL ABOUT ME, ANYWAY?
I...
MY... MY HEART...
I DON'T KNOW WHAT YOU'RE THINKING THESE DAYS, HIROFUMI...
throb
...IT HURTS...
squeeze
MAYBE IT'S JUST THAT...

...YOU DON'T WANT ME ANY MORE?
throb
N-...NO, THAT'S...
TO HELL WITH IT!!
I'M GOIN' HOME!!
VWFF
WHAP
WAAH!
DAIGO!!

thmp
thmp
HEY, DAIGO! WAIT!!
My, isn't this tea good!
Yeah!
DAIGO! HEY!!
thmp
HOLD IT!
SLAM
H--
YOU WOULDN'T EVEN CARE...
...IF I WAS GONE, WOULD YOU, HIROFUMI?!
WH-...

I HATE YOU...!
I HATE YOUR GUTS, HIROFUMI!
ばんっ
SLAM
......
WELL...
WELL, WHAT THE HELL...
IT'S NOT LIKE I KNOW WHAT I SHOULD DO EITHER!!
GOD-DAMN ERK!

AW, MAN, DID YOU HAVE A *FIGHT*, BRO?
NOW, YOU REALLY SHOULDN'T FIGHT!
!!
DAMN IT, DON'T YOU TWO KNOW I WAS BEING ***ASSAULTED*** UP THERE?!!
HOW 'BOUT A LITTLE ***HELP*** WHEN THAT HAPPENS?!!
AFTER ALL THIS TIME, ***NOW*** YOU SAY THAT?
YOU'RE A MAN-- YOU SHOULD BE ABLE TO WITHSTAND THAT.
I SEE...
droop
ぱたん
PTAM
DAMMIT!
THEY ACT LIKE IT'S NOT ANY OF THEIR BUSINESS...
Damn, this room's a wreck.

THAT BOOK BAG...
IT'S DAIGO'S...
I HATE YOU...! I HATE YOUR GUTS, HIROFUMI!!
ずきん
throb
DAMMIT!
WHY'D HE GO AND SAY THAT?!!
キーンコーン
ding dong
AND WHY DOES HE KEEP GIVING ME THAT LOOK...?!!
WHAT?
DAIGO'S SKIPPED SCHOOL?
YEP.
NO ONE'S HEARD FROM HIM. THE TEACHER'S GETTING WORRIED.
And I brought his bag and all...
HUH?
DON'T YOU KNOW FURUBAYASHI BETTER THAN ANYONE ELSE?

.... WHAT THE HELL IS THAT SUPPOSED TO MEAN?
WELL, THE WHOLE SCHOOL KNOWS YOU TWO ARE LOVE-BIRDS, RIGHT?
No!
Tsk!
MAYBE FURUBAYASHI'S JUST SULKING BECAUSE A CERTAIN SOMEONE'S BEEN COLD THESE DAYS?
URK!
Bull's-Eye
You're not s'posed to say stuff like that!
WHAT THE HELL?! WHAT THE HELL?! WHAT THE HELL?!
EVERYONE ACTS LIKE I'M THE BAD GUY...!
YOU WOULDN'T EVEN CARE...
...IF I WAS GONE, WOULD YOU, HIROFUMI!?
throb

NNNGH...
BUT... WHAT AM I SUPPOSED TO DO?
ALL I KNOW ABOUT FOR SURE IS THIS PAIN IN MY CHEST...
AND...
....

KRRRRR..
OH... DAMN IT ALL!
RRRRR...
......
NOT PICKING UP...
MAYBE... I SHOULD DROP BY HIS PLACE....
YEAH... DROP OFF THE BAG... WHILE I'M THERE...

oh!
はっ
BUT, COME TO THINK OF IT...
...I DON'T KNOW WHERE HE LIVES.
dunnn
I DON'T KNOW...
...THE FIRST THING ABOUT DAIGO, DO I...
EVEN READING MY JOURNAL...
...I FELT LIKE I WAS READING SOME FICTIONAL NOVEL.
I JUST COULDN'T BELIEVE THOSE THINGS HAD HAPPENED TO ME...
BUT...
WAIT, I KNOW!!

MAYBE SOMETHING IN HIS BAG...
...WILL HAVE HIS ADDRESS ON IT...
Sorry to go through your stuff Daigo!!
shff
shhp
fltt
HM? SOMETHING FELL OUT OF...
A PHOTO?
WHO'S THIS...?
WOW, HE'S... PRETTY...

WHAT'S THIS GUY GOT TO DO WITH DAIGO...?
HEY... A NAME!!
...AKIHIKO?!
xxxxxx xx, 19xx
Akihiko
THIS AKIHIKO MUST BE...
THAT UNCLE OF DAIGO'S WHO'S MENTIONED IN THE JOURNAL...!!
Gasp
IS THIS WHAT DAIGO WAS LOOKING AT YESTERDAY?!
THEN, JUST MAYBE...

BMP BMP
COULD IT BE... THAT DAIGO'S GONE TO SEE AKIHIKO...?!
DAIGO!!
thimp brump
HIRO-FUMI?!
HIROFUMI, WHAT'S WRONG?!
WHAT? DAIGO'S WHAT?!
DAIGO'S...
THAM

HIROFUMI!
WAIT A SECOND!
skreek
DID YOU AND DAIGO HAVE ANOTHER FIGHT?!
oh!
THAT'S RIGHT...
HIROFUMI!!
WAAH!
LOOK OUT!
queee!

EVEN IF DAIGO HAS GONE TO SEE HIM...
...HUH?
I DON'T HAVE...
...A REASON... TO GO AFTER HIM...
HIROFUMI!!
thakrssh

Waaah...
Waaah...
WHAT...?
Waaah...
Waaah!
SOMEONE'S CRYING...
A CHILD...?
rrsssssh

DAIGO?!
WHY... WHY ARE YOU CRYING...?
oh...
WHY WON'T YOU COMFORT HIM?

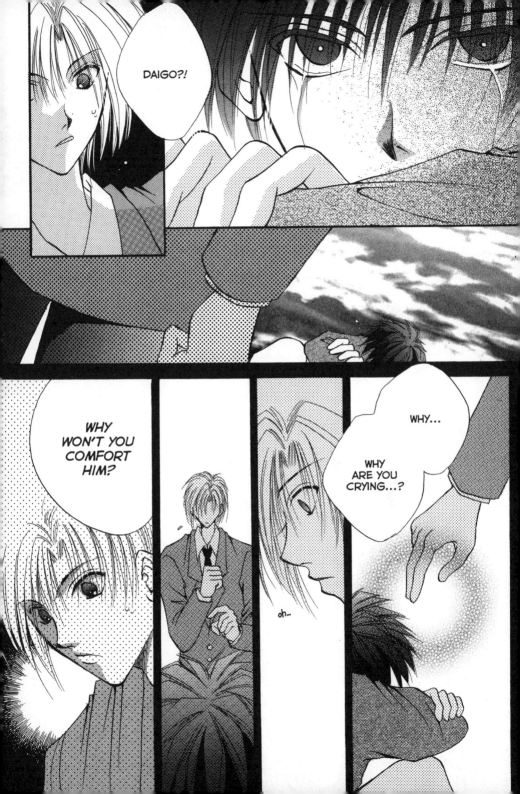

YOU... THE ALIEN?!
And you look just like I do now!
YOU KNOW I'M NOT AN ALIEN-- I'M YOU.
SO, WHY WON'T YOU COMFORT HIM?
I... I DON'T HAVE THE RIGHT.
THE RIGHT?
I MEAN, EVEN I DON'T KNOW HOW I FEEL ABOUT DAIGO!!
HOW SHOULD I KNOW WHAT TO DO WITH A MALE PARTNER?!!

OH, DEAR.
WHEN YOUR MEMORIES DON'T COME BACK RIGHT...
...YOU GET A LOT OF STATIC IN YOUR HEAD AND FORGET WHAT'S IMPORTANT.
IT'S VERY SIMPLE
I'LL SHOW YOU.
LOOK.
HE'S CRYING.
......
throb
YOUR CHEST HURTS, DOESN'T IT?

IF YOU LEAVE HIM BE, HE'LL JUST KEEP ON CRYING THERE.
throb
ずきん
YOU DON'T WANT THAT...
...DO YOU?
THAT'S MORE THAN ENOUGH REASON...
...TO GO AFTER SOMEONE.

GO ON...
GO, MYSELF...
DAIGO IS WAITING.
PROTECT HIS SMILE... HOWEVER I CAN...

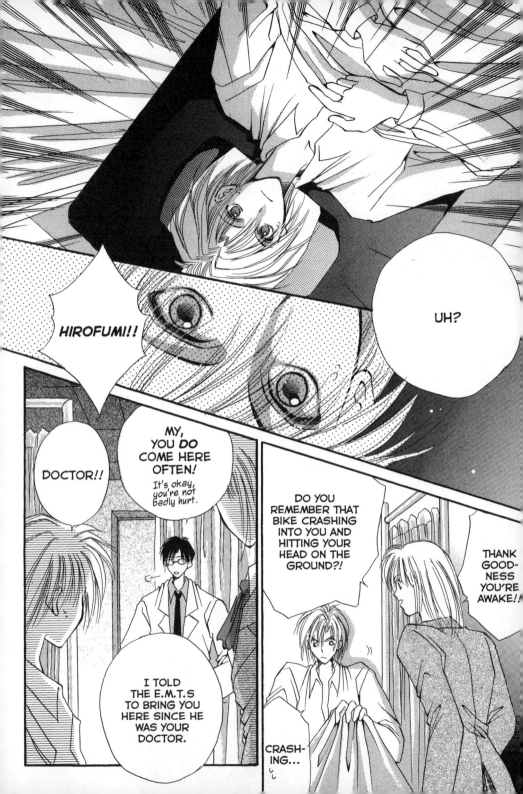

HIROFUMI!!

UH?

DOCTOR!!

MY, YOU *DO* COME HERE OFTEN!

It's okay, you're not badly hurt.

DO YOU REMEMBER THAT BIKE CRASHING INTO YOU AND HITTING YOUR HEAD ON THE GROUND?!

THANK GOODNESS YOU'RE AWAKE!!

I TOLD THE E.M.T.S TO BRING YOU HERE SINCE HE WAS YOUR DOCTOR.

CRASH-ING...

HOW LONG WAS I OUT OF IT?!
YOU WERE ASLEEP FOR A WHILE. IT'S MORNING ALREADY.
DOCTOR!!
Gasp
Y-YES?!
TELL ME WHERE AKIHIKO IS!!
EH...?
AKIHIKO...? HIROFUMI, WHAT...?
I THINK MAYBE DAIGO...
...HAS GONE TO BE WITH HIM!!
YEAH... HE MIGHT BE WITH HIM...
HE COULDN'T BE, HIROFUMI!!

AFTER ALL... AKIHIKO IS NO LONGER AMONG US.
!!
WHAT...?!
I SEE...
SO I WAS OVER-WORRYING ...
THAT'S IT... MAYBE HE'S ALREADY COME BACK HOME...
JUST A MOMENT, HIROFUMI.
ARE YOU SAYING...

...THAT DAIGO... RAN OFF SOMEWHERE?
......
SINCE WE FOUGHT... I HAVEN'T BEEN ABLE TO REACH HIM...
WHEN WAS THIS?
THE DAY BEFORE YESTER-DAY.
I SEE.... THIS COULD BE SERIOUS FOR DAIGO...
どきん...
bmp bmp
WHAT?
EVER SINCE HE GOT BETTER, HE STILL BECOMES...
...A LITTLE UNSTABLE AT THIS TIME EVERY YEAR...

ESPECIALLY TODAY...
...WHICH IS HIS BIRTHDAY...
...AS WELL AS THE DAY AKIHIKO DIED.
!!
I JUST HOPE DAIGO... DOESN'T TRY ANYTHING FOOLISH...
......
DOCTOR...
Silence

PLEASE TELL ME WHERE DAIGO LIVES... OR WHERE HE MIGHT GO.
EH? OH, YES...
AND...
...PLEASE TELL ME...
...ABOUT AKIHIKO AND DAIGO!!
......
WILL YOU ...

WILL YOU... PLEASE GO AND MEET DAIGO...?
......
MY HEART...
MY HEART HURTS...
SO...
......
I SEE.
YOU HAVE A RIGHT TO KNOW THE WHOLE STORY.
I'LL TELL YOU.
AND NOT AS A DOCTOR, BUT AS PART OF DAIGO AND AKIHIKO'S FAMILY.

THAM
"DAIGO'S PARENTS WERE KILLED IN AN ACCIDENT WHEN HE WAS SMALL."
"AKIHIKO TOOK HIM IN AFTER THAT."
......

KLMP
KLMP
DAIGO!!
YOU IN HERE?!
DAIGO!!
COME ON OUT IF YOU ARE!!
KLMP
hmph...
I KNEW IT...
HE ISN'T HOME.
"AKIHIKO HAD NEVER BEEN THE SOCIABLE TYPE, SO HE LIVED WITH DAIGO IN THIS ISOLATED HOUSE...."
"DURING THEIR LIFE TOGETHER WITH NO ONE ELSE AROUND..."
"...THEIR RELATIONSHIP WENT WELL BEYOND MERE UNCLE AND NEPHEW."
"THIS MUCH WAS CLEAR FROM DAIGO'S CONDITION LATER ON."

THFF
STILL FRESH...
...WHICH MEANS...
...FLOWERS!!
"BUT, ONE DAY..."

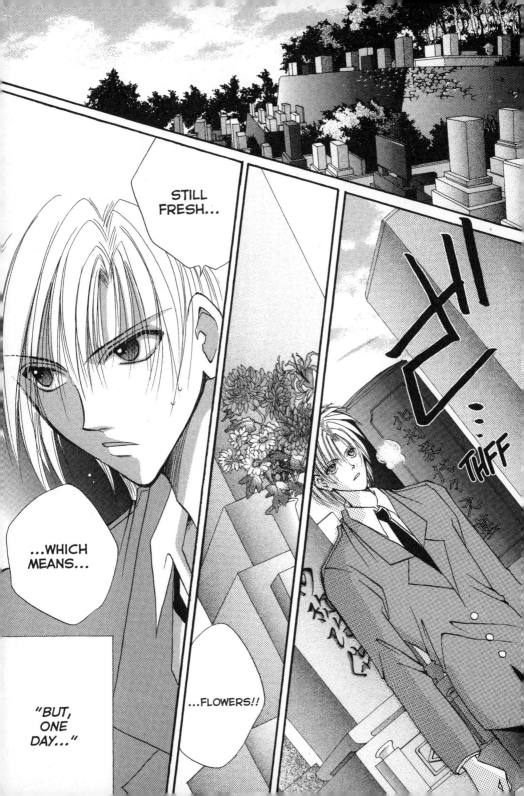

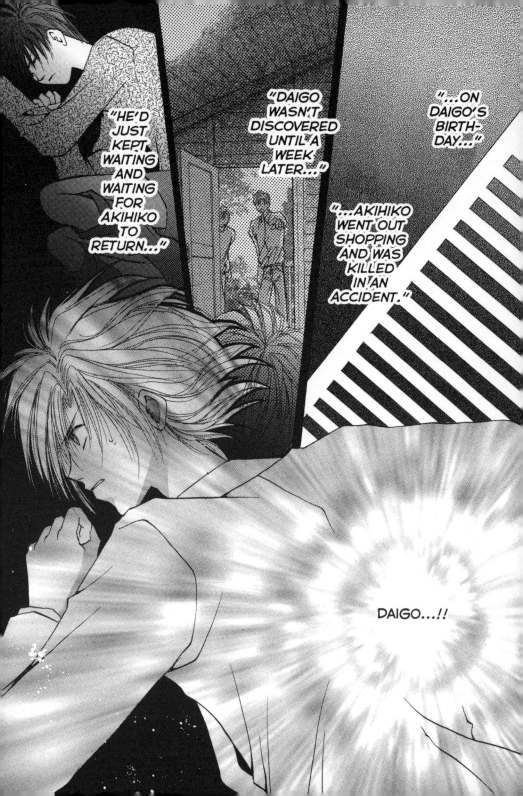

"HE'D JUST KEPT WAITING AND WAITING FOR AKIHIKO TO RETURN..."

"DAIGO WASN'T DISCOVERED UNTIL A WEEK LATER...!"

"...ON DAIGO'S BIRTH-DAY..."

"...AKIHIKO WENT OUT SHOPPING AND WAS KILLED IN AN ACCIDENT."

DAIGO...!!

I FINALLY UNDER-STAND...
...THE REASON BEHIND THAT SAD LOOK OF YOURS.
YOU'VE BEEN WAITING SO LONG, HAVEN'T YOU...
...FOR YOUR DEAREST PERSON, WHO WOULD NEVER COME BACK...
ALL THAT TIME... ALONE ALL THAT TIME...?!
THROB

DON'T CRY... I'M RIGHT HERE...!!

DAMMIT, I CAN'T FIND HIM ANYWHERE!
THPFF
THE ONLY PLACE LEFT...
...IS HERE...
...THE HOUSE WHERE DAIGO AND AKIHIKO LIVED...

ピク…
TWITCH
AKIHIKO...?
NO, COULDN'T BE...

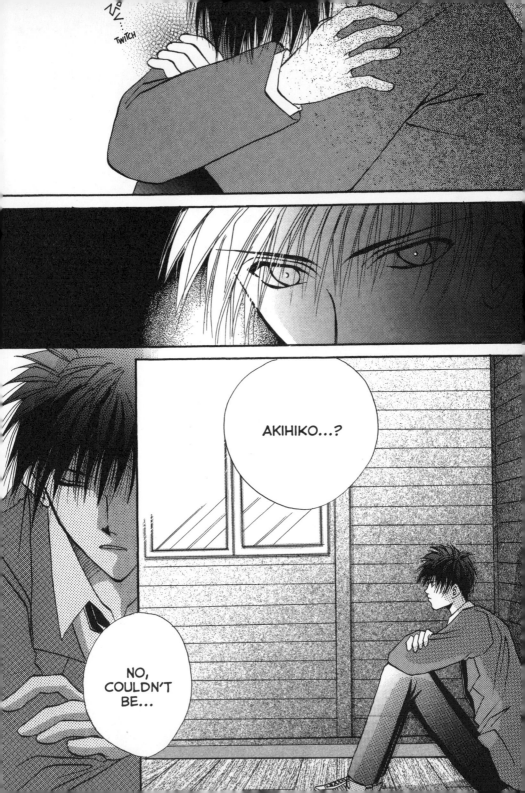

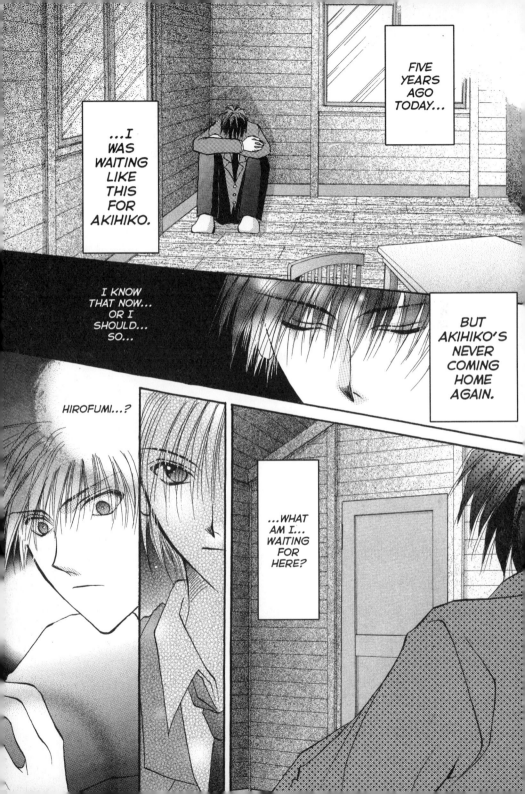

FIVE YEARS AGO TODAY...

...I WAS WAITING LIKE THIS FOR AKIHIKO.

I KNOW THAT NOW... OR I SHOULD... SO...

BUT AKIHIKO'S NEVER COMING HOME AGAIN.

HIROFUMI...?

...WHAT AM I... WAITING FOR HERE?

...YOU DON'T WANT ME ANY MORE?
N-...NO, THAT'S...
HIROFUMI... YOU WERE TOTALLY AT A LOSS THEN...
YOU DON'T...
...NEED ME ANY MORE, HIROFUMI...
THE HIROFUMI WHO BROUGHT ME IN...
...HAS DISAPPEARED SOMEWHERE...

EVEN IF I WAIT HERE...
...NO ONE'S GOING TO OPEN THAT DOOR...
THAT DOOR...
...WILL NEVER OPEN AGAIN...
DAIGO!!

ばん
BAM
WHAT...?
wheeze
SO HERE'S WHERE YOU'VE BEEN...!!
I'VE BEEN LOOKIN' ALL OVER, YOU SON OF A BITCH!!

HIRO-...
...FUMI...
TAP
WHAT ARE YOU...
WHOK
P'UGH!
HIRO-...

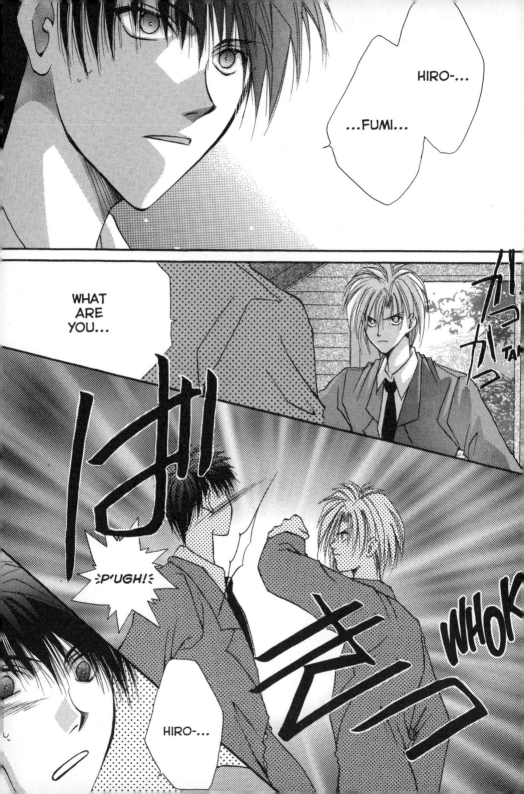

YOU DON'T JUST SIT AROUND ON YOUR ASS LIKE A *SPOILED BRAT!!*
IF YOU LOVE ME, *YOU* GOTTA DO SOME OF THE CHASIN' TOO!!
Y'DON'T GO ALL *COWERING* JUST 'CAUSE SOMEONE'S A LITTLE *COLD* TO YOU!!
Damn coward!!
HIROFUMI...
thff
......

MY HEART...
...HURTS LIKE HELL...
...WHENEVER YOU CRY...
...WHENEVER YOU'RE GONE...
SO YOU'VE GOTTA DO THE RIGHT THING...
...STAY NEAR ME AND SMILE...!!

BAM
COME ON...

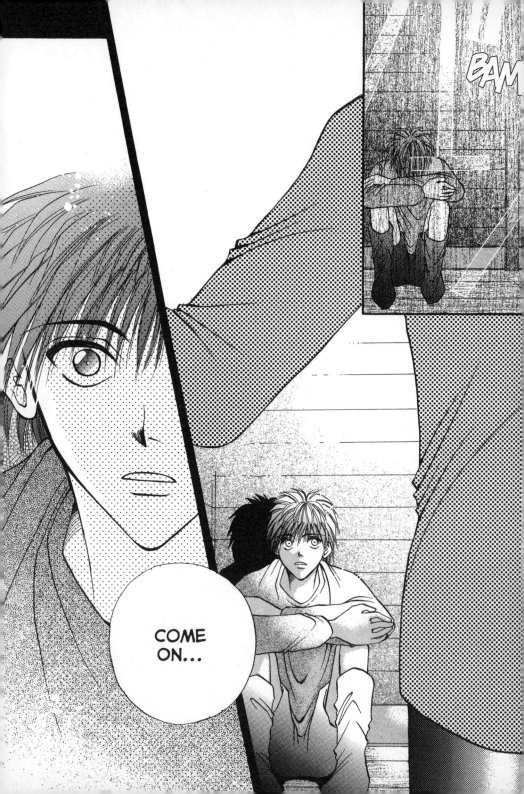

LET'S GO... TOGETHER.

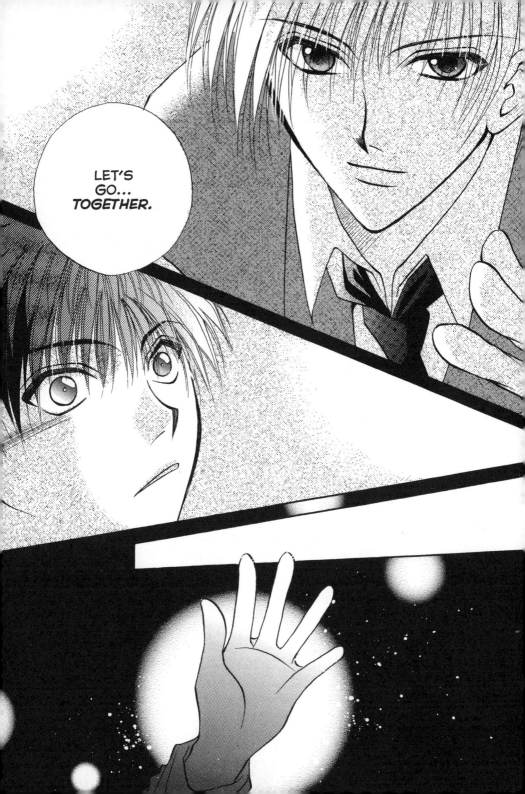

THE DOOR...
...OPENED...
HIROFUMI...!!
WAGH!
WHAT THE HELL?!

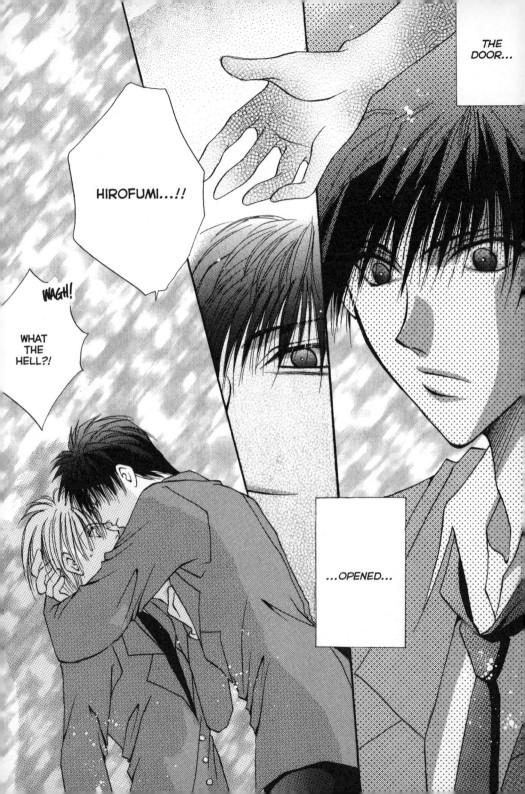

YOU'LL ALWAYS BE THE ONE...
...WHO BRINGS ME IN...
...I WON'T...
...CRY ANY MORE...
......
......
......

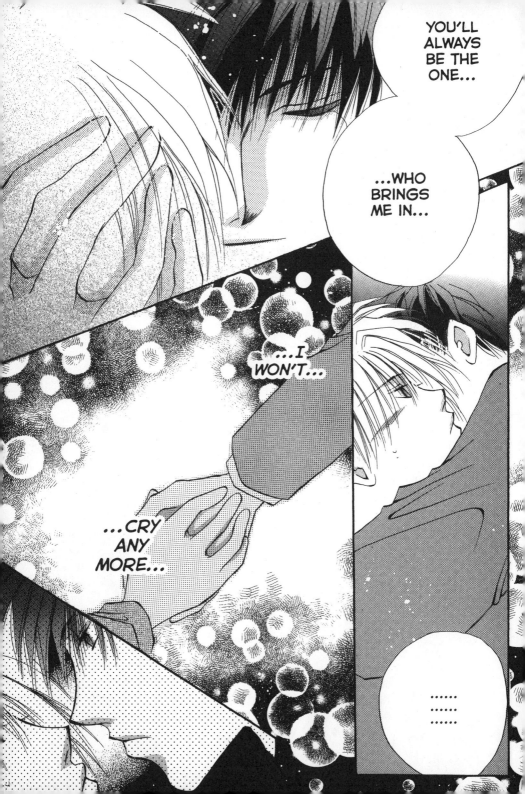

I LOVE YOU, HIROFUMI...
......

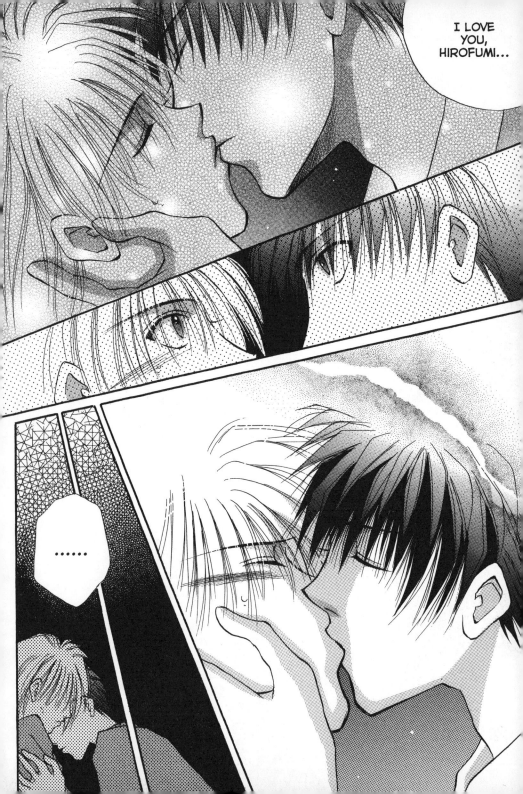

HM?
AREN'T YOU GONNA FIGHT BACK?
!!
WELL, I'M A GUY-- I DON'T SWEAT SMALL STUFF LIKE THAT!!
heh!
OH, YEAH?
Well, then.
WHOA... *WHAT?!*
AAH!
WATCH THE *HANDS,* JERK!!
WELL, HOW CAN I DO ANYTHING IF I DON'T TOUCH YOU?
You're acting like a virgin girl again...
I KNEW IT, I'M JUST NOT GONNA--
I INSIST.
OH, YES, YOU ARE.

DAMN, YOU'RE BOLD ALL OF A SUDDEN!!
Whump
What?
BUT ISN'T THIS WHAT YOU TOLD ME TO DO, HIROFUMI?
"IF YOU LOVE ME, YOU GOTTA DO SOME OF THE CHASIN' TOO!!"
I'LL BE COMING AFTER YOU A WHOLE LOT MORE, HIROFUMI.
'CAUSE I'M GONNA CATCH YOU FOR SURE!!
BMP-BUMP
BRACE YOURSELF, HIROFUMI.
I'M STILL NOT SURE...

...WHAT EMOTION WAS BORN IN MY HEART...
...AT THAT MOMENT IN PLACE OF THE PAIN...
...BUT I DO KNOW...
...I FOUND SOMETHING IMPORTANT TO ME...
I LOVE TO SEE HIS SMILE.
SO, I WANT HIM ALWAYS TO BE SMILING.

DON'T YOU... AGREE?
...YEAH.

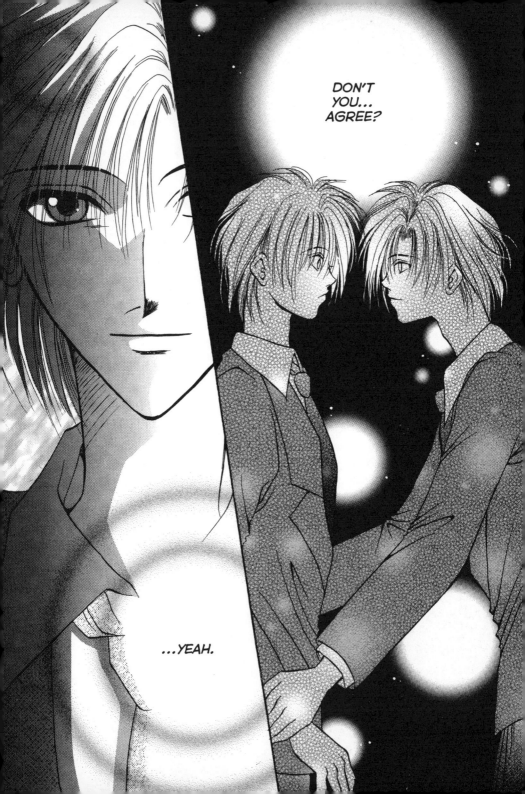

DEAR MY-SELF...
IT'S A LITTLE LATE IN COMING, BUT I'M SENDING YOU A REPLY.

LET'S BOTH... WATCH OVER HIS SMILE FOREVER...
DEAR MYSELF 3 ✚ END

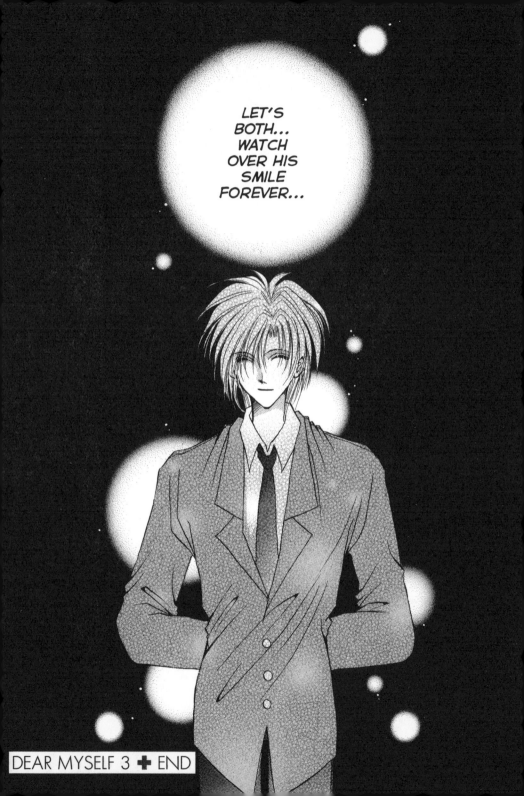

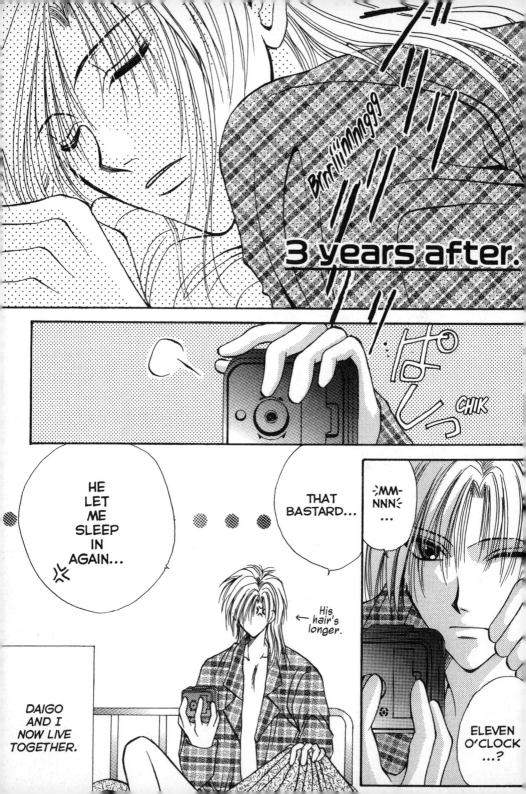

3 years after.

CHIK

HE
LET
ME
SLEEP
IN
AGAIN...

THAT
BASTARD...

-MM-
NNN-
...

His
hair's
longer.

DAIGO
AND I
NOW LIVE
TOGETHER.

ELEVEN
O'CLOCK
...?

YOU'VE BEEN LATE TOO MUCH-- DON'T BOTHER SHOWING UP.
CLICK
......
DUN-DUNNN
DAMMIT, THAT'S ANOTHER PART-TIME JOB LOST, THANKS TO HIM...
Grrrr...
THU FRY SAT
5 6 7
12 13 14
19 20 21
26 27 28
OH!
THAT'S RIGHT.
TODAY'S DAIGO'S BIRTHDAY...
IT'S BEEN THREE YEARS ALREADY SINCE THEN...
SINCE THEN...
NO, DAIGO, WAIT!!
I CAN'T... I JUST CAN'T DO IT!!

IT'S A LITTLE LATE TO BE SAYING THAT NOW!
It's not as if I'm gonna stop!
じゃあ
Whine
ぎゃあ
Whine
IT'S NO GOOD!! WHATEVER YOU THINK, IT'S NO GOOD!! IT'LL NEVER GO IN!! IT'S BIOLOGICALLY IMPOSSIBLE!!
CAN'T YOU JUST TAKE IT LIKE A MAN!?
NO, I CAN'T TAKE IT BECAUSE I'M A MAN!
IT'LL BE ALL RIGHT, JUST LEAVE IT TO ME!!
I'm a pro at this!!
ぎゃあ
FRET
NO! I JUST KNOW IT'S GONNA HURT...!!
ぎゃあ
ARGH
ぎゃあ
WHINE
YOU'RE WASTING YOUR BREATH!!
!!
......
OOH...
See? Told ya it'd be all right....
MY BODY WAS USED TO DAIGO, SO IT BETRAYED MY MIND ALL TOO READILY.
And it was far from painless...!!

ON TOP OF THAT...
DAIGO...
← It looks like they've drowned completely (LOL!)
AH...!
HIROFUMI...
I LOVE YOU...
AIGO...
SLAM
KEEP IT DOWN!!
ぎょ
Yipe!
CH-.... CHIKA!!
I'VE GOT ENTRANCE EXAM STUDY EVERY DAY TOO, Y'KNOW!!
YOU'RE COMPLETELY DISTRACTING ME!!
I hear it all every night!!
We.... we're sorry!
It's not EVERY night! It's every other night!

...I GOT COMPLAINTS FROM CHIKA NEXT DOOR...
...SO I WAS BOOTED OUT OF THE HOUSE WHEN I GRADUATED.
DAIGO'S COMPLETELY BEEN SETTING THE PACE HERE...
AND HE'S GOTTEN REALLY BOLD RECENTLY.
GRRR...
むー
DEAR HIROFUMI: ♥ I'LL BE HOME EARLY TODAY, SO WAIT FOR ME, OKAY? ♥ DINNER'S IN THE FRIDGE--JUST NUKE IT. ♥
AS FOR DAIGO...
...HE ACTUALLY PASSED STRAIGHT FROM HIGH SCHOOL INTO T UNIVERSITY.
HE'S EVEN STARTED UP SOME SORT OF BUSINESS.
CHIKA'S REASONING.
NOT MANY BARGAINS LIKE HIM AROUND.
YOU'VE GOT YOURSELF A GREAT HUBBY, HIROFUMI.
ダンナじゃねえ。
He's NOT my husband.
HE'S BECOME A REALLY PROMISING YOUNG MAN...

I, ON THE OTHER HAND...
...NEVER GOT BACK MY MEMORIES OF THOSE TWO YEARS OF SCHOOL, SO I FAILED MY COLLEGE ENTRANCE EXAMS SPECTACULARLY. I'M NOW A FREELANCE WRITER.
← Practically a gigalo.
silence...
NOT ONLY THAT...
I'LL SUPPORT YOU, HIROFUMI.
...DAIGO KEEPS SAYING THAT AND INTERFERING SO I CAN'T HOLD DOWN A JOB.
I'M ALWAYS QUARRELING WITH HIM AND RUNNING AWAY.
MANY TIMES I'VE THOUGHT I'M GONNA BREAK UP WITH HIM, BUT...
(childhood friend Shigeru Takagishi.)
PUT ME UP, SHIGERU!!
BAM
..... AGAIN?
RUNNING AWAY
I'M ALWAYS QUARRELING WITH HIM AND RUNNING AWAY.
HIS BIRTHDAY, HUH...?
NOW, WHAT SHOULD I DO FOR THAT?
I MEAN, WHAT WOULD HE WANT...?
I'm sure...
EH? WHAT?
WHAT DO I WANT?

(You're lookin' a little old, there, Daigo...)

YOU'RE HERE WITH ME, HIROFUMI ...
WHAT BETTER PRESENT COULD THERE BE FOR ME?
......
the nerve of him, just saying that so glibly.
カーっ
Blush
...HE SMILES AND GIVES ME HIS GREATEST EXPRESSION, SO...

SIGH...
NOT LIKE I'VE GOT MONEY TO BUY A PRESENT, ANYWAY.
GUESS I'VE GOT NO CHOICE.
I'LL JUST GO THE EXTRA MILE TODAY AND GIVE HIM A "WELCOME HOME" KISS.
...TODAY, ONCE AGAIN...
...I'M WAITING FOR HIM TO COME HOME.
3 years after. ✚ END

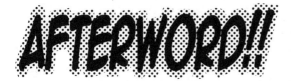

AFTERWORD!!

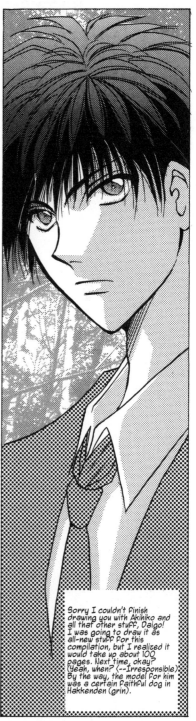

Hello there!! Pleased to meet you for the first time in comics!! I'm Eiki Eiki, a new face in the manga artist crowd!! Yes, the kanji for my pen name are read "Eiki Eiki," not "Eiki Kageki" (I get called that a lot), so please take note!!

Anyway, this is my FIRST comic!! Whee! [♥] At last...at last, my dream has come true!! And it's all thanks to everyone who supported me!! Thank you all soooo much!! (Just keep it coming, okay? [♥] <--Hey!) Of course, right about now, a lot of my dreams (especially about my manga) are coming true, so it's kinda scary. Still, I've dreamed of being a manga artist ever since I was little, so I'm really happy that dream's come true! [♥] After all, I really love manga, so now I just keep thinking how lucky I am to be able to draw it every day. Well, there are occasionally (?) times when I get all hopeless and scream that I'm going on a trip or something. Ah-heh-heh.

Anyway, about DEAR MYSELF.... I actually took the names Hirofumi and Daigo from my beloved little brothers. (grin) My folks got on my case for using my kid brothers' names for a homo couple. (grin) Almost all the other characters' names came from those of people I know. I just gush with affection for the characters when I do that. But I'd decided I was definitely going to use the name "Daigo" at some point. I thought it was a great name, even if it did belong to my kid brother. He's in a band now, by the way, and his hair's all blue-grey. (grin) Now, when this story was running in the quarterly magazine DEAR + ("Dear Plus"), I overshot the page count one time.

Sorry I couldn't finish drawing you with Akihiko and all that other stuff, Daigo! I was going to draw it as all-new stuff for this compilation, but I realized it would take up about 100 pages. Next time, okay? (Yeah, when? (--Irresponsible) By the way, the model for him was a certain faithful dog in Hakkenden (grin).

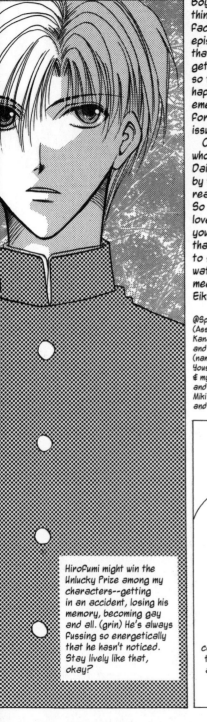

Boy, that was a mess. On top of that, I'd forget all sorts of things in the time between episodes, like how to draw Daigo's face, so he'd look all different from the first or second episode. Somehow his tone got all different too, so I fixed that this time around. And after I'd go to the trouble of getting all the typeset dialog, I'd change things in the roughs so the page count would often run short. (sob) This even happened with the last episode, which made for a real emergency situation, so I had to rush out some additional art for this collected edition. Those of you with the magazine issues, feel free to compare. [♥]

Okay, so, about the new stuff.... I really wanted to do a whole lot more, like the flirting between alien-Hirofumi and Daigo. (It would've been incredibly cool if they'd been okayed by the school.) But....time ouuuut!! Gah, does making comics really take this much time and trouble!? I...I had no idea. So I figured, "Uh, well, I guess I'll just show those two all lovey-dovey as adults." (grin) Finally, I really want to thank you for picking up my half-baked stuff out of all the manga that's out there. I'm gonna keep charging down that road to self-confidence, and I'd really appreciate it if you'd all watch over me with your warm gazes. We've definitely gotta meet again sometime! [♥]
Eiki Eiki '98

@Special Thanks@
(Assistants) Jun Uzuki and Saki Iori
Kanako Sakura & Fuyutou Hitokita & Tatsuki Fujimura and
(name assistance) Kiyoshi Mizui & Chika Igaya & Yousuke Furubayashi & Mayumi Takagishi & Shigeru Kanamaru & my little brothers (grin), Hirofumi & Daigo and
Miki Ishikawa & the WINGS editorial staff & everyone at Shinshokan and you [♥]

Hirofumi might win the Unlucky Prize among my characters--getting in an accident, losing his memory, becoming gay and all. (grin) He's always fussing so energetically that he hasn't noticed. Stay lively like that, okay?

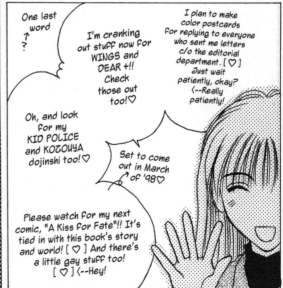

One last word
↑
?

I'm cranking out stuff now for WINGS and DEAR +!! Check those out too!♡

I plan to make color postcards for replying to everyone who sent me letters c/o the editorial department. [♡] Just wait patiently, okay? (--Really patiently!

Oh, and look for my KID POLICE and KOZOUYA dojinshi too!♡

Set to come out in March of '98♡

Please watch for my next comic, "A Kiss for Fate"!! It's tied in with this book's story and world! [♡] And there's a little gay stuff too! [♡] (--Hey!

The Art of Loving

Written and
Illustrated by
Eiki Eiki

OBSESSION

ob·ses·sion (əb-sĕsh'ən)

n. 1. Compulsive preoccupation
with a fixed idea or an unwanted feeling or emotion.
2. An unhealthy, compulsive
preoccupation with some-
thing or someone.
3. Yukata's reaction when he
first laid eyes on bad boy
Tohno.

DMP
DIGITAL MANGA
PUBLISHING
yaoi-manga.com
The girls only sanctuary

Vol. 1 ISBN # 1-56970-908-4 $12.95

Easygoing Kojima, Serious Nakahara...
Will they find common ground?
Little Butterfly
by Hinako Takanaga
DMP
DIGITAL MANGA PUBLISHING
yaoi-manga.com
The girls only sanctuary
PARENTAL
EXPLICIT CONTENT
ADVISORY
Vol. 1 1-56970-907-6 $12.95
Vol. 2 1-56970-906-8 $12.95
Vol. 3 1-56970-905-X $12.95
© 2004 Hinako Takanaga. Originally published in Japan in 2004 by KAIOHSHA CO.LTD.

MY ONLY KING

Created by Lily Hoshino
"The Queen of Yaoi"

Royalty appears in many forms...

DMP
DIGITAL MANGA PUBLISHING

yaoi-manga.com
The girls only sanctuary

By Lily Hoshino
ISBN: 1-56970-911-4 $12.95

TIME LAG

A LOVE LETTER...

Delivered THREE

years later...

Can love bring Satoru and Shirou
together, even after all this time?

ISBN#1-56970-921-1 $12.95

junemanga.com

Time Lag © 1999, 2000 by Shinobu GOTOH and Hotaru ODAGIRI.
All rights reserved. Original Japanese edition
published by TOKUMA SHOTEN PUBLISHING CO., LTD.

YUKINE HONAMI
SERUBO SUZUKI

SWEET REVOLUTION

WHAT CAN BE SWEETER THAN FORBIDDEN LOVE?

ISBN# 1-56970-910-6 $12.95

June™

junemanga.com

Hybrid Child

by Shungiki Nakamura

Half machine...
Half human...
What can your Hybrid Child do for you?

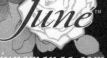

ISBN# 1-56970-902-5 $12.95

Hybrid Child © Shungiku Nakamura 2005.
Originally published in Japan in 2005 by BIBLOS Co. Ltd

Written and Illustrated by
You Higuri
A desperate search…
In the garden of the sacred beast…
Gorgeous Carat Galaxy
Danger awaits those who dare to enter.
ISBN# 1-56970-903-3 $12.95
Gorgeous Carat Galaxy © You Higur 2004. Originally published in Japan in 2004 by GENTOSHA Comics Inc., Tokyo.
June™
junemanga.com

Don't Worry Mama

a novel

Stranded...

Yuichi and his spoiled boss, Imakura, are mistakenly left behind on a deserted island. Can they survive until someone notices they're missing?

One of the most popular "boy's love" stories returns as a novel, and includes a bonus story, "Present."

ISBN# 1-56970-886-X $8.95

DMP
DIGITAL MANGA PUBLISHING
yaoi-manga.com
The girls only sanctuary

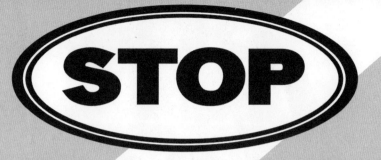

STOP

This is the back of the book! Start from the other side.

NATIVE MANGA readers read manga from *right to left*.

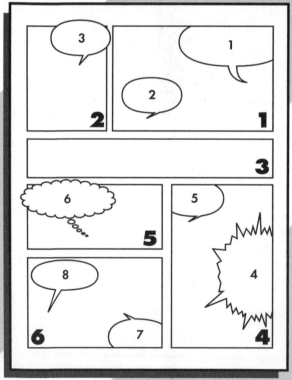

If you run into our **Native Manga** logo on any of our books... you'll know that this manga is published in it's true original native Japanese right to left reading format, as it was intended. Turn to the other side of the book and start reading from right to left, top to bottom.

Follow the diagram to see how its done. **Surf's Up!**

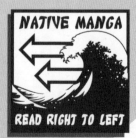

NATIVE MANGA

READ RIGHT TO LEFT